PIECES

PIECES

Putting Life Back Together After Loss

A Love Story

M.L. Davis

Library of Congress Control Number: 2006906521
ISBN 10:   Hardcover   1-4257-2584-8
                Softcover   1-4257-2583-X

ISBN 13:   Hardcover   978-1-4257-2584-6
                Softcover   978-1-4257-2583-9

This book was printed in the United States of America.

Cover Art by Dreamstime.com

To order additional copies of this book, contact:
Xlibris Corporation
1-888-795-4274
www.Xlibris.com
Orders@Xlibris.com
34138

CONTENTS

THE SECOND SIX MONTHS

TO THE READER

This book is a compilation of essays written over a one-year period in my life. The physical act of writing it helped me keep my sanity when my world had gone mad.

Loss of any type causes us to grieve. Often we don't realize we are grieving; we just move on, but something nags at our emotions or puts us in a funk. It's grief. If we name it and pause to look at it, we feel better and move on more healthy than before.

We suffer losses constantly from small to huge: a neighbor's moving away; a favorite family doctor's retiring; a favorite corner store or market's closing; our car being stolen; losing a treasured possession to a burglar; hearing that a distant acquaintance has died. We empathize with strangers who suffer losses in fires or storms or other natural disasters. We suffer through the loss of a much-loved family pet.

The word arrives one day that a close friend is terminally ill, or has died suddenly. We are lessened by their passing. We face the personal horror of divorce and all the awful loss it brings: traditions, values, lifestyles. We lose people in divorces. We are no longer coupled in the same way, and people we associated with, or, sadly, thought were friends, simply fall away. Usually we are better off after a divorce, but it is a loss of part of our identity. If there are offspring, we must see them suffer permanent damage.

We face family illnesses that sometimes are cured; but oftentimes, after valiant struggles the battles are lost. We watch our elderly loved ones fight against the ravages of time; we see their "selves" vanish in the clutches of Alzheimer's disease or dementia or physical weakness. There is the unbearable sorrow of losing a child and knowing that a piece of ourselves is buried for eternity, and the sadness never ends.

Finally, there is the crushing blow of a sudden death of a mate, the soul mate. The person who makes us complete, who knows our thoughts as well as we know our own. The person who makes our heart and soul sing; the person without whom we say we cannot live. Losses. They can gather like vicious demons and bring us down. Or we can choose to know they are there, but refuse to be conquered by them. The latter requires a giant leap of faith.

*   *   *

This book supposes that the reader is a person who has been able to manage (mostly) throughout life; to manage gain, loss, or change of all types. I am not a therapist or doctor; I am a woman who has managed to deal in her own way with the changes life has sent her.

I cannot stress enough the importance of taking care of your health in times of trauma. It's the last thing you think of, but ignoring your needs can cause more problems for you. I learned this from experience. I hadn't slept in three weeks. When I made an annual visit to my doctor, he immediately prescribed a sleeping aid because the body heals grief through sleep. I had not known that fact. When I was able to sleep for eight hours a night, I was able to cope with everyday events without sobbing uncontrollably, and my spirits lifted dramatically. Some healthy food three to six times a day, vitamins, and water help heal the nervous system and build the immune system. If you find yourself sleeping too much, you need to see a professional to deal with depression. Also, if you find yourself binge eating or "grazing" on junk food all day, or drinking more alcohol than usual, curb these tendencies or seek help if you can't. Did you do this before your loss? Then, why start now? Your loved one would not want that for you. Likewise, starving yourself will only add to your problems. This is a time to attempt to do "all things in moderation." Good grieving is a balancing act between letting your emotions run a good course and keeping them in check so they do not control you.

SURVIVOR'S LIST

Take the time to make a list of things you have survived since childhood. They may be small things or huge, life-altering experiences. I found that the list was longer than I thought it would be. Your list may range from surviving the emotional traumas of childhood, to moving away from home, to illness, to financial problems, divorce, loss of friendships, jobs, and loved ones. As the list grows, re-read it occasionally. You will see that you are stronger than you ever believed you were.

*   *   *

PUZZLE PIECES

Commit to doing this activity. I found a favorite photo of myself; one in which I looked very happy. Find a picture like that of yourself. If there are other people in the picture, try to make yourself the center of the photo. Enlarge yourself to an 8 by 10 size. Make two copies of this picture. Find two shoe boxes or containers. Very deliberately, measure and divide the back of each photo into 30 squares. Number the squares from 1 to 30. Now cut the squares apart. Each week, find the correct number starting at one; write one word on the square that describes your emotional feelings that week. Add one more phrase that was some good thing that happened that week; for example, "coffee with friend", or "I took a walk" or "spoke to a friend by phone." Anything positive. After 26 weeks (six months) you will tape or glue this picture back together and begin the process again with the other 8 by 10 photo. In the extra blocks (27-30) write four things: one thing you want to do; one thing you want to stop; one thing you want to keep; one thing you want to get rid of. This activity causes you to focus your mind on something, and at the end of the year you will see that you are still holding together. Like an exquisite crystal vase that has been dropped and shattered, you have been re-fired into a new vessel. You are different, but you are still exquisite crystal. You are still yourself, somewhat scarred perhaps, but hopefully stronger. When you read the words you have written on the back of your photo, you can measure your progression or regression. I wish you progress.

PROLOGUE

Scripture says that the fruit of the Spirit is joy. I have always thought of joy as a gift; some people have it, and some people never get it because they just can't seem to embrace what comes to them. Our gifts often take forms we cannot understand, but the experiences leave us richer for their having happened. This is the story of just such a gift. There will be those who read this and dismiss it as a trite or twice-told tale that they have seen in movie plots or romance novels. On the other hand, there are those among us who believe in angels and know that they do indeed walk the earth. These people know incredible things can happen in ordinary lives, and that the lives touched will never be quite the same. This book is for those people, people who open their arms to the ever-widening circle of life. Life with all of its drama, humor, tragedy, and joy.

THE BEGINNINGS

This story of great joy was born in sadness. A man clothed in sorrow at the loss of his beloved wife would enter my life seeking camaraderie with an old friend. We shared common memories of our children growing up together, very similar lifestyles, and familiar life experiences of religion, politics, fidelity, and family. We had known each other as friends for sixteen years, and it was as easy to listen to him talk of his life and his losses as it was for him to listen to me speak of mine. We understood each other instantly and completely and easily. We could laugh together, and, more importantly and wonderfully, we were never afraid to cry together. We were perfect friends.

Our conversations proved we shared an uncanny compatibility in nearly all things from food, to movies (*Casablanca, Gone with the Wind, An Affair to Remember, The Quiet Man* and endlessly on), to traveling, to music. It was music more than anything else that brought us together. I studied music and sang in a church choir; he had studied music for a lifetime as an avocation and was an authority on the roots of rock and roll. At our first dinner I had played jazz CD's, and as a parting comment wished him "all things bright and beautiful" believing surely that he would be off to find someone to date. Two days later he phoned and arrived at my door with a CD he was sure I would enjoy. As fate would have it, I would become all things bright and beautiful to him, and he would become the music in my soul.

THE LIGHTENING AND FAMILIARITY

I had often heard that when true love strikes, it heralds its own arrival with trumpets, bells, or arias. I was sure that this was movie fiction because I had been married a long time before my husband of twenty-six years opted out. I remember falling in love and knowing that this was the permanent guy, the one I would spend my life with and have babies with and grow old with. Few trumpets, bells, or arias were involved. I loved my husband very much, and I know he loved me as much as he was capable of loving anyone. He was a fine provider and a dependable father to our two children. But he left. And I was forced to create a different me and a new life.

After five years of being on my own, I was very happy with my wonderful adult children and an incredible circle of friends. I loved my career, and after my mother's death at the age of ninety-one, I had loosed the bonds of care giving and begun to enjoy a total independence that I had never known. Nevertheless, somewhere inside me was a numbness born of years of shutting off emotions in order to "get the job done." Whatever the job might be, just call Super Woman; I could handle it all. When a barb hurt, I ignored it until I had quietly closed and locked the windows of my heart. (I really didn't think anyone would ever knock on the door so I guess I left that ajar). Unknown to me at the time, I was harboring a secret fear. I was afraid I would die without ever having been completely loved. (When a man leaves a woman, that's how she feels deep down. Even though I knew intellectually that the man had loved me once, emotionally I was a bereft five-year old deserted on a country road.) Finally, I came to grips with that, and I realized that the "couple" part of my life was over, and I was at peace with myself. Then the Music Man arrived.

After a dinner of flounder that he had caught and had asked me to cook, we had remained at the table for hours listening to music and talking of every conceivable subject. When he was leaving he simply opened his arms and hugged me. Something flashed in my stomach and chest so hard that my knees buckled slightly. I thought for a split second I had been struck by lightening (or at least by a static electricity charge from the carpet). He didn't let go, and we just stood there. He gave me a light kiss and I ducked for fear that I had forgotten how. We laughed and he left. I was shaking like a leaf in a hurricane both inside and out. Trumpets, bells, arias for moviegoers; electrocution and nausea for me!

He called the next day and we began to see each other. He hated being alone, and I enjoyed his company. We both later agreed it was a match made in heaven by his deceased wife and my departed mother. As we came to love each other, I realized I was an open hand, and he was the glove that perfectly fit every curve and crook of that hand, a soft but sturdy covering against the everyday wear and tear of life. The hand was steadying, loving, calming, and giving; the glove was warm and protective and tender. When the hand and glove were together, where did one stop and the other begin? We could never tell. The fit was that perfect.

THE ROOM AND BEYOND

My mind was short-circuiting in the chaos. I was keenly aware of every second from the instant it happened. "I love you more than you can ever realize," he said standing there.

"I do realize it."

"I know, but I love you more than you or anybody can ever understand," he said and he kissed me again. He turned and walked into the next room.

As I stepped across the room, I heard a soft thunk sound as if someone in the next room had thrown something against the wall. For some reason I called his name. There was no response. I moved quickly to the room where he had left the door open and I called his name loudly. I remember that I never screamed. I remained calm, but I kept calling his name loudly. I grabbed his calves and instantly pulled him across the floor to do CPR all the while calling his name and repeating over and over, "No, my Angel!" Don't leave me! I love you, my Angel!" Instinctively, I knew that the hearing was the last sense to go and I think I must have thought that hearing my voice would revive him. His face was so awfully red.

Follow the rules you learned. Clear the airway. Check for breathing. Thump the chest, pinch off the nose, puff twice, clear the airway of aspiration, yes, breathe in, my Love, repeat, run to the phone, 911, run back, thump the chest, pinch off the nose, puff twice, yes, quick cough, my Angel, that's good; again thump, pinch off the nose, puff twice, the door flings open, a police officer is with me, he does the chest and I breathe into him, again, again, again, again. "Breathe, my Angel! You stay with me!" Puff, puff, again, puff, puff, again. We're working together the policeman and I . . . thump, thump, puff, puff . . . noise at the door and EMTs rush in. They lift me quickly from the floor and in one smooth move have him lying in the larger area in the doorway while three of them begin their operations. I grab my purse and instantly read his medical history loudly over their voices. I give them every medication and heart history. They react to all the information and thank me for being so helpful so quickly. The policeman is standing with me at the foot of the bed and he tells me we will be going to the hospital as soon as they can try to stabilize him. I sit down on the foot of the bed.

I am trying to pray. I have always prayed with this man; we have gone to mass together and said the rosary and made novenas together, and I can't remember any of my prayers that I have said every day since I was a child. "Hail Mary . . ." I began over and over not remembering the next words . . . switch to the Memorare, my favorite prayer that never fails . . . "Remember, O most . . .", "Remember . . ." "Sacred Heart of Jesus, I place my trust in Thee!" "Sacred Heart of Jesus, I place my trust in Thee! . . ." "Momma, momma, let me keep him, don't let them take him . . . Momma . . . Hail Mary . . ."

I am trying to remember the words and a huge, soft black woman is sitting on the foot of the bed with me, rocking me . . . I am saying "Hail Mary" and she is swaddling me in her huge arms and I feel as if I am floating on a cloud and she quietly intones, "Sweet Jesus, place this wonderful man in your hands . . . precious blood of Jesus, take care of this good man, Sweet Jesus, bless this wonderful woman, Precious Jesus, we ask this in your name, take him in your arms, Sweet Jesus . . ." "I'm not getting any pulse here," I hear the EMT . . . "Sweet Jesus, help this good woman . . . take this wonderful man into your arms."

Someone says, "we're moving him," and I turn to the woman and kiss her cheek and say "thank you for praying with me . . . who are you?" ". . . I'm the guest in the next room . . ." She squeezes me gently and it gives me the strength to rise and scoop all of our valuables into my purse . . . she keeps her hands on me and moves me to the door and closes it for me and holds me again for a second before I go with the ambulance driver who is telling me we have time . . . we have time . . . I know he's dead . . . if he were alive we would not have time . . . he tells me they are working on him . . . "Is he dead?" . . ."They are working on him . . . we are going to the hospital . . ." the black woman waves me on and gives me a loving smile. I can't remember if she speaks again.

I'm in the ambulance thinking if this is Dallas, I don't want to go to Parkland Hospital. Teenage memories of JFK's assassination. But we are in Plano and Parkland is nowhere near us. I'm strapped in the seat and can't see through the window into the back of the ambulance. "They're working on him," the driver says. But I know somewhere in me that he is gone and this is futile. We arrive and they take him out of the ambulance and escort me to a "quiet room." He is obviously dead because they would not be putting me in a "quiet room" if he were alive. I go with a woman who asks for information. She seems not to be in a hurry and I give her all the information. She says "relationship?" I answer nothing and she says, as she types, "wife." "Wife." That was the future. That would have been. What we have now is "dead." They won't come and tell me but I know. The future is now and it is over, and they won't come and tell me. We were talking and kissing and it is over and they won't come and tell me. "Yes," I say because I know they may not treat him if I am not the next of kin. She escorts me back to the quiet room and the hospital chaplain is there to sit with me. I have done this before and they don't understand that I know the drill. The chaplain tells me the doctors are with him. The phone rings and it happens to be my son who is just calling to say hello and to find out if we are having fun. I report the news that he has had a heart attack and I don't think he will live. My son goes into action and handles all the details of calling everyone.

I phone his daughter and tell her husband who answers to prepare her for the worst. I wait with this chaplain who is asking me if he has a religious preference. I say "Catholic" and in what seems like an instant there is a priest. The doctor enters and takes my hand. "There was nothing more we could do," is what I think he said. And I say I want to be with him. The doctor escorts me along with the priest into the trauma room.

The priest does not pray aloud. He blesses him and makes the cross on his forehead and that is all. My Angel is warm, and I begin to stroke his face as I always did and I try to comfort myself by covering his face in soft kisses. His face, his hair, his nose, his eyes. I say "I love you" into his ear again and yet again. I find tissues and wipe his nose. There are tubes around him that they have removed from his nose and mouth and there is blood on my hands. I turn away and clean my hands. I stroke his face then constantly because he is warm and I want him to feel me loving him to the end. I smile and tell him to rest and tell him I will love him always and I cover his face in kisses again and the priest sees how much I love him and asks how long we were married. I told him we could not get married because we were Catholic and we were waiting for an annulment. He was a widower I say, and the priest's eyes fill with tears because we should have been allowed to marry he says. I smile and cover my Angel's face in small kisses. He is still so warm. I want him to wake up and smile and say this is a prank. And the priest tells me I will mourn this loss for years because he can see how much I love this man, and he is sure we should have been allowed to marry. My hands never leave this face that I have loved. I never hear the priest pray aloud so I say quietly, "May the angels take you into paradise, may Lazarus meet you at the gates of the Holy City." I recite the Anima Christi as the priest listens. "I love you, My Angel." I stroke his hair and study his face and my niece arrives with her husband and they station themselves on either side of me and let me continue to stroke his hair. Medical people arrive with questions and forms and the phone begins to ring with call after call and I must leave his side to do the business of death. I have done this all before and I can do it with grace and ease. This is the fourth time I have prayed over the body and done the paper work. My father, my brother, my mother, now him. One time too many. But I get the job done. He is an organ donor I say. Take the corneas . . . yes, the cartilage . . . leg bones? No, you cannot take his leg bones. I am shocked that they are asking me for leg bone. Don't they know I loved his legs? I loved the scar from his bypass surgery because it had saved his life so that I could love him years later. No, you will NOT take his bones. His daughter calls and she agrees with me. I need proof that I have his medical power of attorney. My son finds and faxes the paper with a cover note that reads "He knew that all glory is fleeting, but that it IS glorious while it lasts. We love you." The nurse reads it and her eyes fill with tears. My son is so poetic she says. I smile in agreement. I sign my name, but this time it is worse than the others; father, brother, mother . . . sudden, sick, very old. But this is tragic. He is not yet sixty. I see both of our names on these papers, but this is the death document. Where is the life document? Did somebody think we lived a lifetime in a year? It was only a year . . . I will count the exact days when I leave this room I tell myself. They want to take him away now, and they slowly gather around in the room. They remind me of a team of lion tamers quietly coming to remove the cub from the mother. They move deliberately as if I may spring on them, but I am proficient at this business of death. And I am polite. I thank them for their kindness and they embrace me as if I am part of the team because I have been composed and easy to deal with. And I pause. I turn and stroke his head and kiss his forehead one last time. He is ever so slightly cooler than he was. And I smile at him. I want him to see me smile as we take our leave of each other. I turn and go with my niece and her husband.

We walk the hospital corridor and drive quietly to the hotel to get the luggage. As I leave the empty room, it is only then that I make the connection from earlier in the evening. He used to say that when he got to heaven, God would be a fat Black woman. The room scene flashed before me and I saw the wonderful Black woman wrapped around me, holding me, swaddling me and I remembered her prayer as I heard "no pulse." "Take him in your arms, Sweet Jesus." That wonderful, comforting warmth; the absolutely serene smile; the unquestioning love; the compassion. And I remembered James Weldon Johnson's marvelous poem "The Creation." ". . . bending down like a Mammy over her baby . . . the great God almighty breathed life into the clay . . ." One of my favorite poems. And I had so often felt like he breathed the breath of God onto me with his love. Suddenly, it all came together: this man who was so spiritual, so ready to meet his maker at any time, so prayerful, so humble, so good . . . this man had seen his higher power . . . . I could not breathe life into him . . . and the only words that God would allow my mind to form were those of acceptance: "Sacred Heart of Jesus, I place my trust in Thee." But SHE was there with me cradling me, rocking me, and talking him into the arms of God. I do believe in angels, and I do believe they can appear when needed. I paused and leaned on the wall. The beautiful Black woman had come to see him home. She was an angel sent to comfort me, and her mission was to take this man to God. How could she have crawled over all those men and their equipment? Why would the policeman outside the door have just let her walk into the room stepping on everybody? Maybe she was no angel. Maybe the face of God is round and loving and feminine and black. If we began in the Euphrates Valley and are created in God's image, are not half of us female? I am suddenly at ease in myself. I am comforted and reassured by the fact that some great thing has happened for this man I love. I believe he has had an escort on the journey to the other side, and I believe I have given him up to beautiful and good hands.

MONTH ONE

THE HUGGERS

When we lose someone suddenly, the shock at first carries us through so that we can gracefully get the body into its resting place. Shock is a valuable commodity at that time. However, some of us are unfortunate in the fact that we cannot cope with the shock itself in order to get the job of burial done. We need extra sympathy for these people because, overcome by the shock, they cannot be present mentally or emotionally for the public grieving, and they should be. They need to remember the outpouring of sympathy for their loved one. Public grieving is offensive to some people. "Have the immediate family" they say. But I have seen enough funerals lately to understand the need for people to come and share their loss. They often are unable to express their emotions because of the suddenness of the death, but it is the actual physical presence of their bodies that is very comforting.

I went to church today for the first time since the funeral almost three weeks ago. I have avoided church, not out of anger, but because I knew what would happen. I went to pieces, sobbing at the sound of the hymns, weeping at the comforting mantra of the ever so familiar prayers. And of course I was at a farewell gathering for a nun who had taught me in high school. We were gathering for brunch at a downtown restaurant after mass, and I had the urge to bolt the church and go home and be alone. But at the end of mass there were hugs. Another dear friend had prepared the way for me by telling everyone that my fiancé had died suddenly a few weeks ago. Few words were needed. It was the physical contact that was so soothing. Having someone's arms around us in a hug is so healing. It is an act of defending us with their own bodies from the firestorm rata-tatting away at us. When they say, "I don't know what to say," we are able to accept that because they are physically present for us, and there isn't really anything they can say anyway. Words really don't take the pain away, but the huggers soothe us; they soothe the anguish with their bodies' warmth. The infant that is cradled feels secure and cries less. So it is with the grieving person of any age.

THE AGONY

How DARE you? Who or what gave you the right to come into my life and WRECK me? What . . . because your wife died of cancer . . . you had suffered a loss . . . . she had told you to go on . . . you wanted to go on . . . you wanted comfort, solace . . . . you wanted to love again?! How dare you. What about ME? . . . I'm supposed to let you love me? . . . I'm supposed to let you "love me like nobody ever loved me"?! And I fell for it. Like a fool, I fell for it. How cruel could you be? You opened me like a gift box, and every day you found some new bit to enjoy, and I let you do it . . . I thought after everything I'd been through, God was giving me my reward for hanging in through all that. I thought I was getting the prize for being good and having done the right things. I thought you were my reward.

I thought we would get old loving each other and holding each other and sharing tender mercies, and seeing both sets of our grandchildren, and traveling, and laughing, and loving and touching, and crying. We would buy a home and throw the door open for everyone to come and share our joy. And you left me.

How could you do this? Why didn't you notice a small pain that maybe we could have seen as an attack coming?! Why didn't you BREATHE for me when I puffed air into you? Why were you so willing to just lie there and die? Why am I God's fool? Why does God think I need so damn little? If you're up there, do you have an answer? Are you going to send me the big sign . . . (probably be a lightning bolt that'll kill me) . . . Are you going to send me some comforter? You know that's really cruel because I don't do the dating thing. That's why I was such a perfect set up for you . . . only one man in my life ever and no one since him . . . perfect set-up . . . say the things I wanted to hear . . . have the same favorite ice cream . . . love the same old songs and movies. How could we have the same favorites? How dare you like everything I like and love everything I love? And politics? How could there be anybody who could love to spar over politics like I did? . . . and agree with me on all the basic issues? How could that happen? And how could you love to have your hand held and your face touched, and how could you love so much how I loved you and LEAVE me? How? You bastard. You precious angel.

I love you so much this might kill me . . . Why? Come and whisper why. Why did I need so little time? Why did I only get fourteen months? Why do so many people get so long . . . they get lifetimes . . . I only wanted about twenty years . . . I thought that was all I could hope for because we were older. Why only fourteen months? Why? Tell me. Somebody tell me.

JUST SHUT UP

I'm really getting tired of hearing that I've "been left with wonderful memories that I can always treasure." And "think that this is all part of God's plan for you . . . we can't say why these things happen, but you have to go on, and all those good times you shared will bring you comfort." That's bull.

When I think of all those good times we had, I want MORE of those good times. Simple. Is that asking too much? I mean, is ONE year in my adult life all I get to feel the love in a great relationship? One wonderful year? Why is that enough? Where do these people who are going home to their husbands of thirty-some years get off telling me that all I need is memories? Can I have a conversation with my memories at my dinner table that is set for one? Can I show my memories the full moon on a gorgeous night? Do my memories put their arms around me when I'm chilly in the movies? Do they fix my coffee and send me beautiful cards for no reason? Do those memories arrive with yellow roses out of the blue just because they love me? Do those memories smile and kiss my fingertips when I touch their face?

Don't talk to me of memories of a man too good to be true. The memories are more painful than I can bear. Just ask how I'm doing, and if I want to talk about him I will. You can mention him, but don't try to soothe me by telling me that I must be grateful for the one year I had. I KNOW that. I understand that. But where do I go now? Grief therapy, right? Of course.

THE DOCTOR'S OFFICE

In 1996, I went to my doctor for my annual visit. As usual he walked into the room and said, "Well, how have YOU been?"

In my usual low-keyed manner (why raise the blood pressure?) I answered this way: "Well, Doctor, there's a rather gross expression in Kentucky where I was born that says, 'my life has turned to slop and the hogs are eating it.' My husband of twenty-five years has moved out of the house, my brother has been diagnosed with terminal throat cancer, my home is up for sale, I'm dealing with lawyers, and I am care-taking my mother because my brother who is dying used to do that. On the bright side my daughter is maintaining straight A's at Loyola University while carrying a twenty-four hour load and living with me through all of this. How's that?"

"Jesus Christ, is your husband crazy? You don't leave twenty-five year marriages! And you need some nerve pills to get through this. How long has he been gone?"

"Since March. I managed to finish teaching the school year with some of the best work I've ever done. How weird is that? But I do feel nauseated most of the time."

"It's your nerves."

In 1997 I paid the annual visit.

"Well, how's it going?" he asked as he came in.

"Well, I'm divorced, my brother has died, my house is still for sale, and I'm spending all my extra time with my mother. Thank God for my teaching job; it keeps me sane."

"You really divorced? That was quick, uh?"

"Exactly six months. He rushed in on a Sunday morning to tell me I had to sign the divorce papers fast or he would be late for 11:00 mass!" I laughed.

"I'm amazed that you can laugh. That's a good thing."

In 1998 I was there again.

"What's going on?" he asked.

"I've sold my house and moved into a townhouse with my daughter."

"Good! Any regrets about the house?"

"Not really. I mean I spent eighteen years gutting it and making it look good, and our kids thought that they would buy it someday, but it's only a house, you know? It was hard to leave it, but it's just "things.""

"How's your daughter?"

"Great! Graduated magna cum laude and is engaged to a precious guy that we all love. Seems like yesterday that you were doing that emergency C-section, doesn't it?"

"How are YOU?" he asked. "Blood pressure is good, blood work is good . . ."

"I'm okay. I'm at peace, and that's a good feeling."

In 1999 I reported in a month late. "My daughter got married, and I moved into my new apartment, a gated community so I feel safe, and I spend lots of time with my mom so I needed to be close by her house in case I need to get there fast. I spend a lot of time with great friends."

"Ever think about dating?"

"Ha! Good grief, no!"

In 2000 we paid our usual visit and I was pronounced "fit."

In 2001 I arrived a few months early.

"How's it going?" he asked.

"My mother passed away in January. I've begun to date a wonderful man who's a widower. He was married for thirty-seven years to the same woman and he was faithful. And I was married twenty-six years and I was faithful."

"Well, it's about time! I want you to get out of this office and have a great time with this man! Your health is great! Go, Girl!"

In 2002 I sat quietly and waited.

"How 'ya doin'?" Your blood pressure is really great."

"Sit down." I indicated his stool.

"That wonderful man I loved has died of a massive heart attack, Doctor. I did CPR, but it didn't work. I think he was dead when he hit the floor really. Right in front of me, there on the floor. Dead. We were going to be married." I stared into space and he was silent.

"You know . . . you've had a little too much to cope with. I'm just so damn sorry."

"Me too. Me too."

"You try to rest and take care of yourself now. Put yourself first. After a while you might try some grief therapy. But just take it easy. Jesus Christ, I'm so sorry. I'm giving you a prescription for your nerves; this is too much to handle. Take care of yourself, you hear? I'm so sorry."

"So am I. So am I."

BREATHE   Bathe   Dress   Eat   Sleep   Visit Doctor   Make Soup

Stop in your reading and devote some time to thinking about how you have been. Jot down your thoughts in the blank pages of this book. The ideas I offer are things that helped me as I went through the grieving process.

In times of trauma we often feel so lost and depressed that we see no reason to leave our bed or dress or eat. "Let me alone!" is what we shout, and then we whimper, "I'm so alone. I can't stand this. I can't survive this."

Breathe. In through your nose; out through your mouth. Deep, slow breaths. Five.

I realized in the hours and days after my loss that I had not been breathing. I was taking in only enough oxygen to survive. I forced myself to take deep breaths, and I was able to be more rational and in control. Pause and breathe deeply a few times each hour. You will notice a difference.

*   *   *

Water is a healing source. Enjoy its simple pleasure. Standing under the shower and letting the water rain down helps tremendously. It relieves stress and clears the thoughts. Look in the mirror. You possibly look exhausted, or puffy, or pale.

*   *   *

Get your make-up. Put on your face.

The person who loved you saw you looking nice. Try to remember that, and try to make yourself look nice every day. If you go to work, you are forced to keep up your appearance. This is a good thing. Wear colors that give you a lift.

*   *   *

Have you let people embrace you? If not, can you say why not? If so, did you find comfort in this? Some of us refuse to allow people to embrace us for fear that if someone does embrace us, we will collapse and lose control. So what? The hugger will understand. That is the purpose of the hug: to support you emotionally when you can't support yourself. Let friends and family know when you need a hug. Just say it: "I'm having a weak moment. I need a hug."

*   *   *

Have you felt any anger yet at your loved one for leaving? Anger may not come until later. It's all right to be angry, but try to understand and tell yourself that we have no control over our moment of death. It is not up to us. What we can control is how we choose to live. Positively or negatively. And whether we like it or not, we are among the living.

*   *   *

Why me? Why not. The rain falls and the sun shines on all, whether they be rich, poor, good, or evil. We are all equal under heaven. This is the awful truth we have to accept, and acceptance does not come easily. Just put that idea in the back of your mind and let it take root slowly over the next few months.

*   *   *

Have you checked in with your doctor? Let him know you do not want to be over-medicated. Avoiding grieving by being dazed with drugs only prolongs the process; or, worse, still, sets you on a dangerous course for a prescription drug-addicted lifestyle. You have to feel some of the pain to know that you are healing. We live in a society that throws pills at everything. If you are totally non-functional, yes, you need some medication. But I have seen people end up with four or five different drugs to take, and they just keep taking those pills for years; sadly, they never address the issue of grief. They don't want to feel any pain. Ironically, they then carry the pain forever. Try not to fall into that trap.

*   *   *

I found myself eating soup twice a day. I had little appetite, and I remembered my mother always had a pot of soup on the stove. This was my comfort food. At first, I ate the canned variety. After two weeks I ventured into the kitchen and made homemade chicken noodle soup. A large pot. I would microwave a mug of it whenever I felt the need. This along with fruit and milk became my favorite meal. I think I was calling on the memory of my deceased mother to comfort me, and she was there in her soup recipe, in the food she had nourished me with as a child.

If you don't have a recipe for chicken soup, buy a package of soup starter. Double its recipe. Add a whole chicken, some chicken broth, vegetables of choice and let it simmer for several hours. Finally, add noodles if there were none in the starter. You now have nourishing food available for several days. Keep soda crackers on hand. Two or three will do wonders for upset stomach.

MONTH TWO

FOUR WEEKS LATER

Sometimes I just want to take my skin off. Tonight I'm horribly depressed. It's Saturday, and I just keep seeing him on the floor. And I want to try to have happy memories with no anger at God. No anger because that would be negative, and I want to remember all the wonderful things we did and know that they were positive experiences for me and for him.

Last night I spoke to his sister who said that she had just finally gotten close to him again for the first time since they were kids. They evidently weren't that close when he was married. Tonight, I keep hearing him say that I had become the great love of his life. When he said it, he paused and seemed to catch himself in a guilty admission. Like he should not have said that to me because he had been married for so long, and he had loved her, and she had died. Then I read his last note he had written to me and I felt less sad, or maybe it made me sadder to realize the magnitude of my loss. It said: "How fortunate can I be to be able to say that you love me! You are such a fine soul mate, so kind, so understanding. I know every day is the beginning of a lifetime of days that we share our love." I'm not sure tonight if re-reading his notes is a comfort. They just make me want him to be here, to come back, to be alive. But he is dead. I know. I saw him on the floor. It's all so exhausting. I just want to go to bed, and pull the covers over my head and sleep and wake up and have someone tell me that none of this happened. That I didn't know this man. That I didn't love this man. That I could pretend I never met him or loved him and it would be easier. I could try to think of ugly things to say about him, but, in truth, there are no ugly things. He was precious and wonderful and bright; handsome and funny and loving and generous; tender and passionate and intelligent and warm, and, always, welcoming. There were no ugly things. Ugly things would make this easy. For some reason God wants to make it hard for me. Really hard. Really, really hard, like beating me in the head with a brick. I keep trying to put my head down so He won't see me to keep hitting me, but He sees me. I can't escape. Why is it that when God does good things we say thank you and give Him the glory, but when He does terrible things we say it was fate? How come we don't hold God responsible for the awful things? I don't get it. I just don't get it.

SEVEN WEEKS

I've hit the wall this time and crashed and burned. I thought going back to school and getting into the routine of teaching would help. It was my help and salvation through all the other things that happened, but this time there is no help it seems. Every day I make it for a while, and then I get this terrible sinking. It really feels like I'm drowning in sorrow; and I've never been an unhappy person. Through everything I've just kept moving and said that God must have a reason. I just can't say that this time. I feel so robbed and cheated, and I feel so dense. I mean I should just pick myself up and get on with it. I know I won't get over it, but I could get ON with it. But I'm just stuck. I had another Woody Allen movie moment: I called a grief therapy group, and they told me they were happy to hear from me and to come to the meeting at 6:30 PM on a Wednesday. I arrived at 6:25 and a sign was posted on the wall: "This building is locked electronically at 6:00PM." There was no access! I just stood there and laughed. Another cosmic message that I did not need help? Then on Thursday, two friends gave me the name of a grief counselor to call. They swore she's the very best. I called. She never called back. And neither did the people from the Wednesday group! I've left messages all over. Maybe I sound too desperate to deal with.

At any rate I have put all of his photographs away, and that is a good feeling. It's just too painful to look at his face and know he's gone forever. I can't get a handle on this "be happy with the memories" stuff. I re-read his notes and I am comforted because I know they are sincere and I know this man adored me. He saw me with his heart, not his eyes. He accepted me just as I am with my wrinkles and cellulite, and he thought I was beautiful. Incredible. "Exquisite" he would say. "With a twenty-five year old smile and beautiful hands". It's almost frightening, but since he died my hands are breaking out in age spots. I feel like the *Picture of Dorian Grey*, and cream won't help. Maybe it's more accurate to say I'm that woman in Shangrilah where the guy falls in love with her when his plane crashes and they are happy and young together, but when they leave Shangrilah she turns into a feeble, decrepit old woman. That's how I'm feeling now. Like I was young, but my turn at that feeling was stolen from me by him when he died. He made me feel like I could conquer the world, but every day that he is gone I feel less and less like that. Sometimes I actually feel myself shrinking. Like I'm being pulled down a corridor very slowly but I can't find anything to grab onto to hold myself in place. I presume all of this is depression, and if one of these professional types would just talk to me I'd probably be fine again.

I managed to host the family summer birthday party! Since so many of us have birthdays in July, August and early September, we have a giant party and all eleven of us blow out the candles. He would have been sixty in July, but instead of him being the life of the party, I put daisies on the table because he liked them so much. It was a great party, but the next day I thought I would drown in tears. I cried like a fool for about three or four hours. I've given parties alone for six years, and I will continue to give parties alone. And furthermore, I know that there are millions of widowed and single women out there who have normal, happy lives. I know because I AM one of those women. I was alone when I was married, I was alone when I was divorced, and I'm alone now. He was an awful yet wonderful accident. Wonderful because he made me feel loved and wanted and so secure. Awful because he came to my door and disrupted what had been a contented life, and I resent that in some way.

And that's where I am seven weeks and a few days later. Sometimes maybe we're better off not knowing the great stuff that's out there. I mean my big fear after my divorce was that I would die never having been completely loved by a man. Now I've been completely loved by an incredible man for such a short time that it was only a tease for all the great things we had planned. Probably better never to have had that than to have this awful pain. It was too short. I knew he said he was on borrowed time, and he told me every day that we had to make today count because it was all we were guaranteed. But I think we both believed we had at least five or ten years because he felt healthy. And I could have lived with five years. We even discussed that. We would be able to say that it was five great years, but it was not to be, and I am left to wonder why. I am left to accept what I cannot change.

EIGHT WEEKS—THE GIFTS

When you hit the bottom, there is no place to go but up. I was at my lowest ebb at seven weeks, three days. The following evening I went to dinner with a dear friend, the next evening with a high school chum and her male companion. They were leaving for New York on September 5, and I encouraged them to enjoy each moment as we had done last September. (We had arrived just in time for autumn in New York, and the World Trade Centers had been destroyed by terrorists the week before). What I found soothing was the fact that they are the same ages as we were and they are just as in love. Madly. I could understand so readily everything they were feeling, and I could only rejoice for them.

Something in me is relieved now when I see lovers. I know I haven't missed anything in my life, and I find that comforting. It doesn't make me sad or jealous. I know how they feel, and I had never known that before. That is a gift. The three of us discussed all this at dinner, and my friend mentioned that she gets terrified every now and then that her companion will die suddenly as mine had. I told her not to think that way. I told them what the man who loved me had taught me: live this day; give up the worrying about things you cannot control; nothing happens by accident; it is meant to be.

I felt so much better when we parted company. I had actually been able to make them feel reassured in their relationship, but the purpose of the dinner was for them to comfort me. They did. Just seeing them was like seeing the reflection of the two of us in a mirror. Yes, I miss him painfully, but to know what perfection we had shared in our relationship is truly a gift, and seeing these two only reinforced that. I felt lighter than I had in weeks.

BREATHE   Do Tasks   SMILE   GO OUT   RELAX

Stop reading and ask yourself what these essays meant to you. Add your thoughts.

Are you angry with God? It's okay. Tell Him how angry you are. Out loud. Go into a room alone. Have a long talk and unload on Him. Yell at Him if you want. You'll feel better after you do this. Talk to Him often, yelling if you have to. The more you talk to Him the better you begin to feel. You're making contact with Him in any way you can, and you have every right to be furious. If you talk to Him daily, you actually begin to feel less angry.

*   *   *

If you have children around, arrange for someone you trust to take them out for a time so you can be alone to cry and vent your anger. Showing children some emotion is good and normal. Showing them too much, too often, can frighten them. Children have a way of forcing us to be brave. We try to keep ourselves together for their sakes. But talk to them and share good memories of the deceased, and let them talk to you. Don't force them to say more than they want. A few words at a time are adequate communication. Hold them in embraces that soothe them. If they reject this, remember that they are often afraid of losing control and crying. Grieving isn't cool to a preteen or teenager. If you understand this, it makes your job easier. Have a relative or friend that the child is close to speak to them. They may be afraid of adding to your burden of grief, so they bottle up their own. A few family therapy sessions can let children know they are okay and what they are feeling is normal.

*   *   *

Do you have a minister or spiritual director to visit? They can offer insights we may overlook.

*   *   *

Go out with a friend and talk about some pleasant time you both shared with your loved one. Smile.

MONTH THREE

WHY WE NEED PUBLIC MOURNING

September 11, 2002 came and went with a huge national day of mourning yet again. I personally think it was too much television in the faces of families who were trying to grieve their individual losses. It was overkill to our psyches to see so much pain over and over. However, I have now seen both extremes.

On September 12, 2002, my dear friend who had shared every event in my life for the last twenty-four years died of cancer. The end came quietly in her own bed as she wanted it, and Hospice had handled the final weeks. I ate dinner with her and shared a laugh on Sunday; on Tuesday she did not know me, and she was dead on Thursday. I had accepted the inevitability of her death as she had, and we rarely spoke of it. We did not avoid the subject; but we had exhausted the topic over the years because we discussed everything in depth. She was a doctor's wife and widow, and when the diagnosis was pronounced,she knew the outcome. She had said she did not want a huge funeral, but she added that we could do what we wanted. Unfortunately, I think her children took her a bit too literally, and there was no service of any kind. This has left many people at loose ends. I see the beauty now in having a public grieving. It is cathartic and soothing. I know from experience.

When my father, brother, and mother died, they were buried with beautiful services. There was a mass with music and singing, there was a eulogy, and in my brother's case, a Marine honor guard and a piper who played "Amazing Grace." Yes, people were brought to tears as well they should have been. Lives were finished, and the endings needed to be noted. After the interments, everyone was invited back to the house for food, liquor, and celebrating. We celebrated the life of the loved one we had lost. If we have the right to life, we certainly have the right to have its ending noticed. Recently, when my companion died, four hundred people signed the book at the funeral home. Four hundred people came to pay their respects to a man they had known as a fellow worker, father, volunteer, fisherman, and friend. Again, the mass was said, the music was played, words were written and spoken, and the body was laid to rest. Though I was devastated, I was soothed to know that he had been loved by so many people. And friends came home with me to further celebrate his life, and we cried and laughed together. We all felt better though we had suffered a terrible and sudden loss.

Having no service leaves the story unfinished. When my friend died on Thursday, there was a staggering silence in her home. The ten people gathered made no sound of prayer or weeping, as though those things were somehow prohibited. On Sunday there was a tiny gathering of twenty people, and no one mentioned her. No toasts were made to her memory, no words spoken. Today twelve of us interred her ashes, and, yet again, there was silence until the Our Father was said. There were no songs for this woman

43

who loved music. There were no words for this woman who had grandly written herself across the pages of our lives for so many years. So tonight I am at loose ends, as though there is unfinished business somewhere. It is as though she passed out of this world unnoticed and unnoted, and I am upset because her life was worth noting. In deference to her children, her closest friends complied with their way of doing things. It will be to our own detriment. We did not have that public time of gathering and weeping and laughing about the antics of our dear friend. We will grieve privately, but it is public ceremony that puts closure to lives and deaths. We remember the ceremony, and that memory finally helps us accept the fact we cannot change: the person we loved is indeed gone. And when we have low moments, we are actually comforted by remembering the final gathering with its outpourings of sympathy and kindness and love and tribute. We are somehow adrift without them. If we are all players on the stage of life as Shakespeare says, then the life well lived deserves to be noted with a round of applause, a "bravo," or a standing ovation.

ELEVEN WEEKS—THE RING

He pledged himself to me every day, and I pledged myself to him. We renewed our vows each day and thanked our God and higher power for giving us to each other. We were gifts: I to him; he to me, and we found new depths of feeling as we unwrapped our true selves on every level. Our joys in each other were boundless, and our discoveries made us as giddy as twenty-somethings.

One day on a foreign shore in what I can only describe as a fantasy, he officially proposed. He did it in his own inimitable style. He bought himself a beautiful black coral ring. I was rather surprised because he did it so quickly. Saw it; tried it on; bought it. I was at another counter buying myself a necklace and earrings. He came to me and showed me the ring. It was beautiful on his hand, a gold and black ring on that bronzed skin I loved. He casually asked me if I had seen a ring I liked. I said I hadn't looked. He pointed to one and the associate took it from the case. I said that it was beautiful and unusual. He said, "If you'll have an unemployed, broken down guy on borrowed time, I would love to marry you."

I think some sort of wheeze sound came out of me as they told me to put the ring on. I was so stunned! After what must have been a pregnant pause I said, "You're retired, you're not broken down, you're not on borrowed time, and of course I will marry you." We all laughed and he kissed my hand and I kissed his. The associate thought we were terribly romantic.

After completing paper work we were out in the setting sun heading for a nearby pub where we could wait while they sized my ring. I was babbling and giggling and we kissed in the street and I was sure we were starring in a great movie. As we drank iced tea and the sky grew orange, he asked the waitress to take a photograph of us, and he stuck out his hand. "Get my engagement ring in the picture," he said. It is a wonderful snapshot of two very happy people. It was early March, spring was in the air, and our hearts and souls were in bloom.

By June we had decided that we would set a wedding date for sometime sooner than later. We didn't know when, but we knew we wanted to be together every second we could find. Our love was so definite and matter of fact that it still leaves me breathless on occasion. We would marry, buy a home, and enjoy our grandchildren (he already had four, and I was expecting my first). We discussed the paper work we would have to do involving separate property, but we were not about property and material things; we were only about each other. But some things that could be bothersome never have to be faced; they are tomorrow's issues, and tomorrow is not guaranteed.

So today I returned the ring he had bought for himself. It was to the New Orleans branch of that jewelry store where I had enjoyed my fantasy afternoon. We had visited this local branch of the store in mid-June to meet the designer, tell him our engagement story, and show him our rings. The old gentleman was so delighted to see his designs on our hands. I had the option of buying the ring or returning it. I have no need of his ring though it is beautiful; I only have need of the hand that wore it.

I thought it would be easy to part with it. It was only a ring after all. As I handed it over, that awful and familiar pain arose in my throat. I had told myself there would be no emotion. Of course, when am I right these days? My stalwart angel daughter was with me and she hugged me while I cried briefly. The store manager brought me water, and asked my permission to give me a hug. It was a wonderful hug, and she is a warm and endearing human being. She made an extremely difficult task less so. I signed the paper work and we enjoyed the manager's company for a while. When we left, I had the feeling I had just donated some body part without benefit of anesthesia. God . . . it was so painful. It made me exhausted.

I had thought about his ring several times since he died. We had agreed that they would be combination engagement/wedding rings, so keeping it was important to me. I treasured my own ring, so I thought of making his into some other piece of jewelry that I could wear, but the shape of it did not allow for much other than a pin. I kept looking at it over the weeks, and I kept putting off a decision.

Then I realized he was trying to tell me something. I read it in one of his letters. "I have no need of material things. Only the tender mercies you so lovingly render." Then I heard him say, You don't need a ring to know what we had." No, I don't NEED the ring. But it was a reminder that we had had a wonderful plan in mind: we were going to spend the rest of our lives together.

And on July 5, an evening in full summer, we sat in a swimming pool and quietly spoke of how incredible our relationship was. How completely we loved each other; how loving at our age made every moment seem important simply because we knew time was not stretching endlessly before us. How we had seemed to connect at the soul and intellect as though we had been together forever. How we knew what the other was thinking. How we loved looking at each other across a room of people when we entertained. (He would do a quick wink, and I would return a smile knowing we had made a roomful of people comfortable). How we loved the life that we were building. How beautiful he thought I was. How handsome I thought he was. How I loved his face with its lines and creases; his strength of character and his wonderful soul. We said all that in the pool. Quietly. Lovingly. He ran his fingers over my neck and shoulders as we watched a flock of birds entertain us zooming from tree to tree.

"I absolutely adore you," I said. "I know you do," he answered. We left the pool and strolled back to our room. He opened the door, put his arms around me, kissed me and said, "I love you more than you can ever realize. I can't explain it to you or anybody because I can't even understand it." We kissed again, and he turned and went into the next room. And he took his leave of me and of the life that we were making in this world.

No, I do not need his ring. I will keep forever the real things that it symbolized. What we had was intangible. I have the gift that will never end: the knowledge that I was loved completely and in every way by an incredibly wonderful man who chose to spend the rest of his life with me. And he did.

BREATHE PRAY or MEDITATE COOK FOR FRIENDS GO OUT

Recite a favorite prayer or mantra several times a day. I found that my childhood prayers were of great comfort. At first when I prayed I became hysterical. After a while, prayer became a source of peace and strength. Sometimes I found that having a conversation with the person I lost was helpful. One-sided, but helpful. As I soothed myself with prayer, I began to notice things that I perceived as messages from the man who had loved me. These coincidental things comforted me tremendously, like a gift from above. I felt he was close by, only in another form, and that he was giving me strength to carry on. Have you had such an experience? Are you soothing yourself with prayer or meditation or music? It is in the quiet that we begin to find ourselves again. It is in the quiet that we hear the voice of God. Listen.

*   *   *

As you deal with the business that comes in the aftermath of death, try to give some thought to positive memories. It is easy to become overwhelmed with the tasks at hand, and most people who surrounded you in the beginning have gone back to their normal routines. Cook a meal for those people who have been so supportive of you. Nothing shows affection like food, and they have probably brought you several meals. Thank them by taking care of them for an evening. What will you cook?

*   *   *

If there are personal belongings involved, have a close friend help, but don't rush this if you don't have to. Let some time go by before you deal with things that cause emotional reactions. When my own mother died, her belongings stayed put for nearly a year before we could cope with their disposal. You can deal with this when you are able. If you have to move to a smaller place, which often happens after a death or divorce, call a friend to "walk through" with you. This is a time when a close friend may have to "strong arm" you a bit to get the job done. The friend will be thinking more clearly and can make lists of things you "must" keep, "may" keep, or "can't" keep. Call friends and offer them a souvenir of "can't" keeps, or donate them to charity or put them up for sale. (Remember that sales can be tedious work and often bring very little money).

*   *   *

Listen to the friend's advice while you make your lists. Write down his or her suggestions if you are not able to assimilate everything at once. (Grief has a way of playing with the memory. You don't want to have to call this person three times to repeat the suggestions to you.) Envision your new dwelling, or think about how you may want to re-furnish or re-furbish if you are staying put. A simple coat of paint can do wonders for the environment and give you a psychological boost. It will occupy you, and at this time being busy is a really good thing.

MONTH FOUR

THREE MONTHS GONE AND THE STORMS HAVE COME

Sometimes I think I'm backpacking through Hell. I was naive to think that this would get better as time passed. It seems to get worse. I have good days, and then I come home and wonder what will become of me. I tell myself I am just going to go on like I did when my husband walked out. But this is different. This man adored me, and I adored him. And he is not here.

The causes of all this angst are two storms: Isadore and Lily. In the last week of September, the city was inundated with twenty-four inches of rain. It was only a rainstorm, but it angered me. I was angry because I was alone. It was no big deal really; it was only rain. But I was alone in a tropical storm. One week later Hurricane Lily was categorized as a Category Four heading just barely west of New Orleans. A Four. We live in a saucer, and a Category Four hurricane would cause thousands of deaths and total destruction of one of America's most fascinating places. I remained calm and told everyone I know to pray to Our Lady of Prompt Succor. Of course, in this city of sin people pray like crazy all the time. My daughter wanted me to stay at her house, but she did not want to insist that I leave my home. So I decided that this was a demon I had to face by myself. I would stay home alone. It was my first hurricane alone actually. I had either been at home with parents, married, or with children. I was absolutely terrified deep inside myself. I think the fact that I am without a partner again really hit home to me. No one to grab when the electricity goes off (and it did go off for a bit), no one to lean on if water begins to rise (it did not), no one to sit with as the deadly calm comes just before the blow (that's one of the really nerve-wracking parts of a hurricane), no one to hang on to as the winds howl unmercifully in the trees and the rains pour down. He is gone, and I miss the physical presence of him more than I can begin to describe. It is an unfillable emptiness in my home and in my being.

I thought I was doing pretty well, but just beneath my surface is a rage that is tremendous. Not at anything in particular, and not at God, and not at him. Just a storm within myself; my own hurricane. That stillness that I can't quite decipher as exhaustion or depression, then the rage of nerves wondering what will happen to me now, then the quiet time when I tell myself it will all work out, and finally the flood of tears that comes unexpectedly and leaves me either tired or exasperated with myself. I get exasperated because I know I am going through what every human being goes through when a loss is suffered. I am not special. Realizing I am not special only makes me feel worse because the person who believed I was so very special is gone. If he had loved me only half as much, this would be only half as painful.

THIRTEEN WEEKS: THE DONUT HOLE

I'm trying to write my way out of this. I watch kids try to talk their way out of things every day, and I smile; and on a good day I am amused and on a bad day I want to say, "Talk yourself out of THIS hole if you can." Every day I think things will get better. I get up, I go to work, I cope with all the usual things that go on at work when you work with 150 twelve, thirteen, and fourteen year olds. Actually, their personal chaos is comforting in so many ways. It removes me from myself; it amuses me to overhear their jokes and conversations; it forces me to be calm because they are always in a dither about some minor thing; and, it makes me focus on my subject material, or, as importantly, their serious problems that crop up on any given day. So I am going to analyze this problem of mine just as I would any other. My dear, dead friend Ruth always said I had no emotions; I had ice water in my veins she swore. She was always emotional; I was removed and able to see both sides of any issue. I'm *trying* to see both sides of this one. This is where I am this week: in the donut hole.

Imagine the most delicious donut you have ever tasted. The donut represents all the delicious things surrounding me, both past and present. I am surrounded by incredible memories of a man who loved me, and by a wonderful present tense filled with my own fabulous children and great friends who are my oxygen supply, a job I really love, and a soon to be born grandchild about whom I grow more curious each day. There is nothing wrong in my life at this time. So why am I positive that I am that incredible shrinking woman who is becoming invisible? I am hanging on to the sides of the donut, but I can't seem to pull myself up. I'm afraid I'm going to fall off because I'm losing my grip on the sides. For some reason I feel like people are leaving me. (Understand that I keep myself occupied constantly by going places with friends). I am beginning to feel cut off when I walk into my home and I am suddenly alone. Actually, I used to enjoy the feeling because at work I am never alone for a second, and closing the door at the end of the day was a relief from racket and confusion. But that silence was chosen. This silence was forced on me.

When he was here, there was a fullness to the place that I can't seem to recapture. He made my life much larger than I ever imagined it being. We saw so many of the same people I still see, only I am alone again. I was alone for six years with them, but it was different. I was alone not by choice, but I was nonetheless determined to make my life the way I could be comfortable with it. *La femme seule*. Of course, I was stifled in my efforts by my mother, who at ninety-one required a great deal of my time. When she passed away, I felt relieved of a much-loved burden. I was finally birthed into my own identity. But I did not have time to get used to that identity because he entered my life two months later, swept me off my feet, and recreated me into the most cherished and fulfilled woman I could be. I was certainly never expecting that; I had planned to be alone. It was a year of incredibly focused love and attention. It was he who noted on September 11, that, in the final analysis, we are not important to the world, only to each other. After that, we loved even more intensely because we both realized that time is so terribly finite. All we really are assured of is Now.

When I plan my days lately, I put the pen aside and ignore making a list. I seem to be wandering in a circle afraid to plan a full day because I know how a day can end in a shattering second when someone hits the floor and is dead. It ends that fast sometimes. And maybe that is too fast. I think of the last lines of Shirley Jackson's story *The Lottery*: "You didn't give him enough time to choose! . . . It isn't fair! It isn't right! . . . and they were upon her." They were upon *me*. Those angels of death pulling him away from me as I desperately tried to breathe life into him. But the fiends angelical had their way. Of course, he *won* the lottery. He died exactly as he wanted, quickly with no suffering. That was wonderful for him. And I should not take this personally. We all know that lottery winners are selected at random, no rhyme or reason.

So why am I afraid I'm going to fall? The donut is reality; it is what I have. If I fall, I may lose touch with the wonderful things that fill my life. As much as I sometimes want to let go, I know intellectually that I have to hang onto those great and good things (including his memory) that surround me. I think of myself as an experiment: I know I could go to the doctor and get a pill that would make me feel happier. But I want to see if I can write my way out of this. Less emotion; more logic. The problem to solve? A heart to mend. A hole to climb out of. And I'm hearing Mya Angelou's sonorous voice, "And still I rise; and still I rise."

FOURTEEN WEEKS: ROOM ASSIGNMENTS IN HELL

So much for writing my way out of this. I have to adjust the metaphor I used before. I said my reality was the perfect donut. I was afraid to fall and lose my grasp on my wonderful reality. But this week I've realized that I'm falling off the donut and there is nothing to grab. I have read somewhere that people who suffer loss often want to stay immersed in the past and think only of the lost loved one. Not me. I'm busy from dawn to midnight, and I am surrounded by all good people and things. I don't think of him endlessly, I don't pine away for what I had, and I don't go around staring at his pictures wishing he were here. I keep moving, and the big revelation came about an hour ago when I got teary-eyed for no reason while driving down the street. I am the dog chasing its tail; I am moving and making no progress.

It is the *lack* of him that is completely overbearing. The lack of sound, the lack of words, the lack of simple touch, the lack of humor, the lack of commentary, the lack of godliness. To love another person is to see the face of God. And I always saw God in his face. Now I can't see God. I know He's here. I get that concept. But when that man looked at me, I knew God loved me, and it was an incredible discovery for me. And, yes, I can do the old "find God in everyone you meet" trick; and yes, it's often true. But not like it was with him. I was just so *sure* of him. I had never been so sure of anything in my entire life. Finally, I had the tune, the melody, and the rhythm all together in perfect harmony. I was loved totally and completely just as I was. So, I've been assigned to the hole. That perfect donut is just a bit too far above me, and like Tantalus, I hunger and thirst, but I am not allowed to eat. Quite a severe punishment. But a perfect analogy for this depression into which I have been exiled.

Who am I to think I am too strong for medication? That is false pride, so God is bringing me down again. Breaking me once more so I can understand the weaknesses of others by discovering my own. If memory serves me, I believe Lucifer is frozen in the ice in the ninth circle of Hell. His sin was betrayal; perhaps mine is pride; pride is the ice in my veins. I have always resented people who walk around with long faces refusing to see their happiness and creating a hell of sorts for others. I think I resent them *more* now because they are fools who have no idea of what they are missing as the seconds tick away. But I have a whole new understanding for those poor souls who want desperately to be happy and cannot be because their brain chemistry does not allow it, and the medication they want so much is out of their reach financially or medically. I admit it. I have a problem and I need help. Intellect tells me to see the doctor on Monday for an anti-depressant. Emotion tells me I need more time to grieve. They are both right, but intellect wins again. I refuse to let pride stand in my way. Life is short, and it is for the living.

ADDICTION

I think I am becoming addicted to sorrow. I go about my business, then, I cannot resist the impulse to be sad. Silly things bring it on. Today, I opened the mail, and there was an envelope from Continental Airlines. My earned miles. It was like a punch to the nose. Whap! He's dead. Whap! He's gone. Whap! All the trips with him are finished. Whap! Whap! Don't bother to get up. Whap! Down again. Punching me, screaming at me. Dead. Gone. Whap! Exhaustion. Nobody wants to hear about this anymore. Friends get on with their lives, so I try not to mention it because I don't want to become a drag that people regret seeing. They might say all I do is whine and pity myself. Not really. I have a ton of things I'm upbeat about, but I keep coming back to the loss. The phone doesn't ring as much anymore. People used to call constantly because they wanted to cheer me. Now they presume that time has passed and I'm back to my work routine and they see me socially, so all is well. Whap, whap. On the floor with no one to pick you up. Pick yourself up. Wipe the blood off your face. Tell it to the computer. Others find the bottom of a liquor bottle or a pill bottle. I see now how those souls get lost in their addictions. But I know there is help. They don't believe there is. I admit I need help. They can't admit it. That is the only difference between them and me.

SIPPING AT THE LETHE

The doctor has prescribed medication that I am to take for one week. He says I am suffering from heavy grief caused by the loss of more than one loved one. The medication will get me over the hump and allow me to focus on something other than sorrow. I am an experiment again. First, I was writing my way out of this. Now I am writing my way out with the help of a medicine that, supposedly, will allow me think of something besides the loss. I have taken it twice, and I am certainly not feeling better yet. I am watching myself going through the process, and all I can think of is the newly admitted member to Hades sipping the waters of the Lethe River in order to forget about the living world. I am completely lethargic. I don't feel sad; I just feel tired. The doctor said to give it one week. I have five days to go.

THE MEADOW AND THE MOUNTAIN ROAD

On day three on the medication journey I actually felt focused, and I accomplished several tasks. It was a gorgeous New Orleans day, one of those perfect October beauties low in humidity, bright in sun, cool in breeze. Perfect. Every day when I finish the hard news and editorials, I read the comics and horoscope for fun. On Saturday the horoscope said to "expect the unexpected." I was not expecting to feel so much better so quickly, and it was a fine feeling. I went to dinner and a movie with a friend, and I noticed I was a bit less talkative than usual. I didn't quite know what to make of that, but all in all, the day was a success. Not so with day four.

I think the horoscope is twenty-four hours ahead of clock time. The "unexpected" must be that I was certainly not expecting to feel completely and totally depressed today. I mean pack the parkas, people, that winding road down to the ninth circle of hell gets really cold! I just hope I don't meet Lucifer face to face. It has been a very scary day. I have felt numb and sad, but underneath that is a fury and rage; the storm is churning in me. And I went to dinner with a dear cousin who came in from out of town, and it was exhausting to be sociable. When I got home, I thought I had done a day's work. This was really unexpected.

I keep wondering what the lessons are in all of this. I have said over and over today, "Just take care of me, Lord." Somewhere in me I know God is breaking me again. Today it is because I have always secretly resented the unacceptable. The unacceptable behavior of students who refuse to learn from their mistakes, the unacceptable behavior of adults who refuse to be happy, the unacceptable behavior of addicts who refuse help, the unacceptable behavior of anyone who should know better. So I must accept the unacceptable. I must accept the death of the person who loved me; the person who let me know that life was truly fantastic, not just wonderful, but truly fantastic. Maybe I'm being punished for lying to God. I mean I say the Serenity prayer every day several times, but I must be insincere. "Lord, grant me the serenity to accept the things I cannot change, the courage to change the things I can, and the wisdom to know the difference."

Well, I know I can't bring the man back to life. I tried to save his life, and that didn't work. Maybe CPR is a pride thing. It makes us feel god-like to save someone. Maybe we should be like those people who stand by and do nothing. Then of course we'd be blamed for doing nothing. They would scream at us, "Why didn't you try to save him?!" And we would answer something pithy like, "What? Do I look like God to you?" I presume I have courage to change the things I can because I am attempting to get on with my life, and I hope I have enough wisdom to know the difference between the two. Of course, there are those who would say, "Enough already! Get a grip on this and knock off the whining." I'm really trying not to whine. I try to hide and lick the wounds very privately and quietly. So I have to accept the unacceptable and the absurd because I have no control over God or the wretched Atropos and Lachisis. One measures; one cuts. And they quietly snicker at me as I wander down the mountain road and the storm rages within me and the temperature drops rapidly. Maybe God will save me before I reach the ninth circle. I have always believed my father's favorite expression, "God and I against any two." I know He's out there. I just can't see Him or feel Him or hear Him now. I feel abandoned. I always tell students that God will never abandon them because He takes care of sparrows and they are more important. Maybe I've never believed anything I've told them. I thought I did. But He's crushing me for some reason. Maybe it's for lack of faith. Lots of "maybes" today. Maybe I'll never make sense of the absurdities. Maybe this medicine is really affecting my mind.

TRAVELER'S AID

Somehow I have been able to pull off the road as I was winding wildly downhill and spend time at a rest stop. As hoped, the Lord stepped out and caught me in mid-plummet. I am reminded of the old story of the man who drowned and went to heaven and asked why God hadn't saved him from drowning; God told the man He had tried to save him three times. He had sent a truck when the rains began, a boat as the waters rose, and a helicopter when the house was under water. The man refused all the help God had sent. I guess my truck came in the form of a pill. Prayer was my boat, and God was the Rope.

I did notice one thing at the rest stop. I was totally silent as a writer. I went from terrified to numb to quiet. I replaced writing with reading. I read a fine small book called *Come This Way* by Mary Jo McCabe. It deals with life on the other side. I have long believed that there are people among us who can communicate with those who have crossed over or died. I think these people are given this ability by God to help the living grow in faith and know that death is not an ending, but only a new dimension. I do think that many of these people are charlatans, but I do think that some of them are touched by God. At any rate, I have been silent, and it was what I needed to be. I have been healing my spirit. I am beginning to know that the silence is not emptiness, but rather stillness. There is a great difference. Emptiness brings on sadness and depression. Stillness brings a calm with it. I can be still and feel a certain contentment I haven't had until now. Of course, I pray very often. Little mantras like, "OK, God, help me with this . . . get me over this minute . . . let me get this done . . ." It works. I am amused because psychologists say we turn into our mothers. My mother had all these little prayers like the ones I just said! Well, everybody loved my mother, so I guess if I can keep the best of her alive in me things will be fine.

I gave up the pills after two weeks and returned the unused portion to the doctor. There was something about me that I was not totally comfortable with. I felt sedated. I was still. I was thinking, but I was deflated. But I was making it. So, I decided that prayer and work would suffice for me because I just wasn't comfortable with being numb. However, what finally puffed me up this week certainly did not come in pill form. On October 25, I was at lunch with my son and daughter-in-law celebrating her birthday. We were in a great little Thai restaurant, and the waiter noticed it was a birthday. He said he would like to give us dessert. Well, when the dessert came, I had an incredible moment of knowing that the angel man who had loved me was still very much with me. Out came the waiter with strawberry ice cream surrounded by bananas! Stunning! This was his and my favorite ice cream and bananas were his favorite fruit. I just smiled a huge smile, and I realized that the little book I had read was true; our loved ones do not end, they move on to another dimension and are eternal as we have always been taught. I found that very comforting. Since then, I have felt more like resuming my trip. It seems the weather is clearing and the scenery is much nicer.

BREATHE   GET HELP   STAY in TOUCH   DETERMINE to LIVE

Survivor Guilt and Anger

Write a response at the note section to these thoughts.

Have you had more bouts of anger or guilt? These are rational feelings. Do you find yourself asking

Why did you survive and your loved one did not?

Why did your loved one suffer through a long illness only to die?

Why did your loved one's death come with no warning or reason?

There are no answers to these questions.

The man who loved me told me often that we are put here for a mission, and when the mission is accomplished we leave. For those of us who are left behind, it is a hard concept. But since we are never privy to the answer, perhaps his theory was as good as any other.

Accepting what we cannot change is difficult, but we will surely ruin what is left of our life if we make acceptance impossible. What we have to do is try to accept without becoming bitter.

Bitterness diminishes the love you shared with the one you lost. This is one of those times when it is best to put a smile on your face and fake it until you can accept the following truth: our fist-clenched arms are not long enough to reach the jaw of God.

MONTH FIVE

WAIT! WAS THAT THE QUEEN I JUST SAW?

*T*he man who loved me promised me that one of the great events of my life was lying just ahead. We anticipated it giddily together and talked of how we would have to create time for a new routine in our schedule. But when the day arrived, I was alone and desperately wanted his hand to hold. I know he was with me in that hallway. I could feel his arm around me and see his smiling face. The rest was glory.

*   *   *

We were always up for a road trip together, and we covered vast amounts of territory from coast to coast. I told him we were on our journey to Ithaca. "Ithaca" is one of my favorite poems, and C.P. Cavafy got it right when he said we must stop at ports of call and gather sweet perfumes along the way. We gathered the sweet perfumes life offered us every day. Now I'm on the journey alone, but I still look for every wonderful thing I can find on any given day, and what a treasure has been handed to me today!

It is a gorgeous late October day, and I receive a phone call at work that says if I don't want to miss the event I must rush, or I will lose the once in a lifetime opportunity. I call in a teacher to substitute and nearly fly to my car. Wow! As I drive, my imagination takes flight . . .

I have read about this for years! How people can be standing around and suddenly without warning she appears. Now someone has told me a piece of insider info . . . she's on the way . . . perfect photo op . . . something to tell friends about . . . ("So sorry YOU couldn't have been with me, deary . . . Ta ta,luv). I arrive. There is a Christmas-morning anticipation among the group. She appears. The crowd suddenly moves itself as one body, fans chasing their idol. Flashbulbs begin to pop, the glare is blinding, and the hisses of the advancing films are anything but vicious. We are friendly and loyal and adoring paparazzi. This queen is among friends. We watch. We attend. She moves out of sight, and we brag to each other about how lucky we are to have had this opportunity. The crowd disperses, but it occurs to *me* that she must come back the same way she went, so I quietly retrace my route and wait. I think of how long I have admired her and loved all that she represents, and I wait. I want to tell her how I feel about her, about her whole wonderful family, about how courageous she is for having made this trip through uncomfortable circumstances in order to greet us, and I wait. And suddenly, as quiet as the star rising in the East, she is coming toward me. Just me! She has only one attendant. They stop. I am dumbfounded at the awe of the moment; I am speechless! She is smaller in person than one expects, but she commands admiration. I bend as anyone should upon meeting her. "Is this your first time?" her attendant asks. I nod and smile because tears are inexplicably pouring down my face, and I smile even more! And she should be called Wonder, Counselor, Emmanuel, born to make us more than we ever hoped to be. The circle of life is repeated. The power of love continues. "Then I'll let you be the first to kiss her. Say hello to your granddaughter."

THE GRAND CANYON

I first flew over the Grand Canyon on my way to a wedding in Las Vegas. My fear of flying had to be set aside so I would not miss the opportunity of seeing one of the world's great wonders from the air. I forced myself to look down after climbing over two friends to get to the window. A short glance was enough for me. Splendid to behold, but not my idea of a good landing strip (logic does not apply to the fear of flying). On the return trip it was dusk, and I was preoccupied with getting home so I did not bother anyone with an attempt to get to a window. How things change in a year!

"Look down, my love," he whispered. I leaned over him and he put his arm over me like an angel's wing. With him I had no fear whatsoever of looking out of plane windows. "See the colors in the rock? The purple and pink? Look how the orange seeps through to the top." He would do a watercolor for me he said.

"Look at that single tree growing out of that rock." I sounded like a kid on a discovery field trip only I was far less cynical. Many teenagers are too busy being sophisticated to be impressed with incredible sights of nature, but not I. (Guess that's why I'm the teacher, but I digress). Of course, I admitted to him that I had missed the gorgeous colors on my first trip. It seemed only brown or orange at a quick glance. The fine nuances went unnoticed because of my fear.

Fear makes the world small. "Fear is the bulldozer of dreams" is what one of my former students wrote once. "Fear is the bulldozer of dreams." But I had put fear behind me now. I had my Big Angel's wing around me, and sometimes I could swear we were flying without a plane; up where the air was rarified on a glorious flight of fancy. My eyes devoured the gaps and crevices, and at thirty-five thousand feet the thing still looked huge, and it was a sight to behold. We decided then and there to do another trip. We would fly out and rent a car.

I have come again to this grand canyon; this place of breath-taking beauty and silent danger and sudden death. Only this time I am alone, and the canyon is in my mind's eye. Some time between Then and Now, the trip's itinerary changed. I went from being a woman madly in love and planning her own future in a state of thrilled delirium to being alone again and a grandmother. It's all been too quick for me to grasp. So I am crossing the chasm. I tell myself over and over that I cannot let fear overtake me. Fear is unfaithfulness to him. He feared nothing, and for me to become fearful is to deny what he created in me. He gave me the love I had prayed for for years, and fear diminishes love. I am running across the gorge as fast as I can. Behind me is the happy lover I was *supposed* to be; ahead of me is the wise older woman I *am* supposed to be. Beneath me, crashed on the rocks, is What Might Have Been; and since I dare not fall into there, I am running. I presume it is a leap of faith I am making, for I am jumping, not from rock to rock, but wing tip to wing tip. My children, my family, and my friends have all lain down for me. They have covered the jagged rocks and allowed me to use their backs. In doing so, they are saving me. Far more importantly, without their knowing it, they have turned themselves into angels.

BREATHE SMILE HUG LAUGH   WORK READ VISIT PRAY

Moments of joy, (weddings, graduations, births), continue among us even in our grief. Try to seize on these occasions to see that life does go on—differently—but on nevertheless. Never turn down an invitation. Even if you are feeling as low as a snake's belly, get dressed and go. This keeps you in touch with life. Do you resent special occasions, or enjoy them? List some special occasions that have occurred since your loss and how you felt about them.

Fear kills. What are you fearing the most and why?

Live in the moment and fear falls away. Are you staying in the moment? There is a difference between living *for* the moment and *in* the moment. "*For* the moment" indicates you believe there is no future. "*In* the moment" indicates that you are focusing on being aware and connected to what is happening at this moment. You are willing to enjoy and live every experience. The poet Goethe wrote: "Nothing is more important than this day." If we believe that, we begin to find a new depth of faith. We also begin to cope. We are not fearing tomorrow. We are living today.

HOLIDAY SEASON

HOLIDAY SEASON

I haven't written since my grandchild was born. I went into what seems to be a state of overdrive, and I cooked every night for the new parents for two weeks, and then Thanksgiving was upon us. We gathered at my home as we did last year. It was just a bit different.

Last year we were all dizzy with my happiness. My children had prepared the side dishes as we had gone on a spectacular trip to Charleston, and we returned home only the day before Thanksgiving. We gathered and giggled and took wonderful, smiling pictures of us all and the day was glorious. We discussed the upcoming Christmas holidays.

This year I prepared the meal, and everyone arrived, and the focus of our conversation was the tiny angel baby we had been given. I smiled and wore my game face and actually enjoyed the day. I was fine in the evening after everyone had gone home and I was alone with the quiet. The next morning I went shopping with my daughter as is our custom, and I was fine that evening. The next morning I awoke and was so depressed I could barely breathe. I moped and wept and wept again. The content of the thinking was "woe is me . . . what is to become of me . . . I am so alone . . . I miss him more than I can bear . . ." and I told myself it was okay to feel this way. I called a friend and left the premises. I returned to the emptiness, but I felt a tiny bit better after talking with someone. I decided to have a party.

Now having a party may sound strange to some people, considering it was the last thing I really wanted to do, but I set the date for the seventeenth of December. It would not be my usual annual cookie exchange. It would be a small dinner gathering for only my closest friends who had spent time with the two of us during our year together. The closest friends numbered around thirty. (God has been astoundingly generous to me in the friend area. I think He knew that since He would take the men in my life away, He would give me a circle of friends to be my salvation). I composed a letter and gave a copy to each friend there. It was a thank you dinner really. My gift to them for having given me the gift of themselves in my time of desperation. The tree was up, the lights were strung, the ornaments were hung, and my home said "Christmas" but in a bit quieter fashion this year. Everything is a bit quieter.

The Christmas concert I sang this year was merely something I promised the choir director I would do. It was beautiful as usual, and as fate would have it we were positioned in the choir loft this year rather than on the altar. It was fortunate because twice during the concert tears poured down my face as I sang. It's amazing to me that water pours out of my eyes at certain phrases of a song. "Be near me, Lord Jesus, I ask Thee to stay close by me forever and love me I pray." Tears all over my face! And of course, last year there were ten guests of mine in the congregation to listen. The man who loved to hear me sing was chief among them, and we took the guests back to my home for dinner after the concert, and it was a wonderful day of laughter and warmth. This year one close friend managed to be there, and since she had to go to work, I went back to an empty house and cleaned. Very different from a year ago.

The days passed quickly, and Christmas Eve was upon me. For the first time in my life there would be no activity at my home that night. I gave my children my blessing and told them they could do as they pleased and visit other relatives and friends. I would sing midnight mass with the choir as usual. So I dressed and went to my son-in-law's parents' home. It was a delightful evening, and I love how his family loves me and includes me. (God has been astoundingly generous to me in the in-law area. I hear people complain that they don't get along with the in-laws, but I have a daughter-in-law and a son-in-law that I consider my own. They are both precious to me, and I am grateful for them every day). It was soon time for church.

I was not really up for the event, but Mozart was to be sung with eleven pieces of the philharmonic orchestra accompanying us. I tried to stay in the moment so I would not think of this night last year. My daughter says that midnight is too late for mass, but when the lights are thrown off, and the candles offer the only glow in the church as the violin plays "Silent Night," Christmas is born again for me. And, yes, I weep and wipe my eyes and pray that the re-born Baby will bring us all peace for our souls. The mass was beautiful. I arrived home and I allowed myself to think of Christmas past.

I snuggled up on my sofa and re-read the beautiful cards he had written to me last year. There were three regarding Christmas. He thanked me for making Christmas a month long celebration of family and friends and music, and it made him love the holiday again. I read them several times and I relived the moment when I opened the box and saw the diamond earrings he had given me. I cried tears of joy that night when he said, "They say 'Diamonds are forever;' just like our love." I cried tears of healing this night. They weren't sad or depressed tears; they were tears springing from the knowledge that I had been loved completely. My tears were comforting to me because I know he would have been on the sofa again with me if he had had a choice. He wanted to be with me always, but God was not to be astoundingly generous in that area. Of course, we did have *always* if we consider that the amount of time we were allotted was our *always*. I finally fell asleep at dawn and woke at ten to drive to my sister's home ninety miles away. We all gathered at noon and the day was very nice. I say *nice* because there was a bit of emptiness in each of us that our new tiny angel could not be expected to fill. I wore a smile, determined not to bring anyone down on Christmas. My main gift of the day was an opportunity to sit in a quiet corner for two hours and hold my granddaughter while she slept. I thought of nothing. I was at rest listening only to her regular breaths as I cradled her close and rocked. My new role in life had been presented to me, and with a spirit bowed, but not broken, I accepted it. I had made it through the day, and I was thrilled with myself. Tomorrow would be another story.

I awoke at my sister's and made coffee and cried like a fool. I wallowed in my weeping! I wailed loudly because the house was empty and I could not embarrass myself! I loved it!

I laughed through my tears! This was just a safety valve gone off; all the tensions of the day before and the brave front could be pushed aside. A hot shower made me feel like a new woman. After an enjoyable lunch with my sister and brother-in-law, I returned home. That evening I went out with a friend to see a movie, and it was a pleasure to be with her. The next day my time was filled with my daughter at a bridal shower and luncheon where I met a woman who had been born in Kentucky as I had. We hit it off immediately; it is so good to meet and make new acquaintances. The next day brought the wedding.

I had my hair done, bought a periwinkle silk suit, and set off. It was the same wedding reception we had planned for ourselves . . . on a beautiful French Quarter patio . . . very New Orleans . . . an authentic jazz band providing the music . . . very New Orleans . . . slow dancing with a jazzy drag . . . good food . . . good friends. I made it through the ceremony by remaining focused on the moment. I avoided hearing the words of the minister as he spoke of lifetime commitment, of love, of memories to build. I chatted with my Kentucky pal and mingled with other familiar faces. When the band played "New York, New York" and "Do You Know What It Means to Miss New Orleans" I suddenly saw myself dancing with him. Right there. It could have been our wedding. Time to leave. Keep smiling. Keep moving. Get the car at the garage. Get in. Lock the door. Put on sunglasses. Breathe in through the nose. Let it all out with a huge loud "UGH!" Be quiet. Breathe again. Be still. Be calm. Smile. He would have been here if he had had a choice. Comforting to know. Go home, change clothes, meet friends at a restaurant to celebrate their thirty-second wedding anniversary. Thirty-two years of being together and creating history, but not perfect years. Ups, downs, the normal day -to -day routines that wear us all either away or smooth. And I smile. I smile because they tell me I had perfection. Fourteen months of perfection. They are right. It is comforting to know they saw it too. To know I had not dreamed it. To know it had really happened. Perfection. Onward! To New Year's Eve.

Last New Year's Eve we were on a mountaintop in Gatlinburg with his sisters' families. It was zero degrees outside, and he had sketched the hills into his sketchbook. A small charcoal rendering that I treasure. We talked of what a wonderful year it had ended up being. Awful beginning for him, but a happy ending. The completion of my mother's life at the beginning for me, but a happy ending. We were so content. So filled with joy. So grateful to God for putting us together. This New Year's Eve I marched off to my grandbaby's house, determined to baby-sit while her parents went to an afternoon movie. She and I had a good time. We strolled, I fed her and rocked her; she slept in my arms, and I bathed her and fed her again. She was so adorable! I left there and drove to my daughter's house to hug them. That evening I went to a formal dinner party with friends.

Midnight on New Year's Eve can present a problem for a single woman on a porch with four married couples. You have to wait your turn to be kissed Happy New Year on the cheek by everyone. Those first few seconds when everyone is kissing, you just kind of stare up at the sky hoping to see some fireworks to occupy your eyes. Surprisingly, I felt okay with the moment. As we all hugged and kissed, I stayed in the moment and enjoyed it. We turned our attention to flashes in the sky, and my dear friend put an arm around me, hugged me, and she began to cry. I told her I was all right; I told her it was comforting to know that he would have been right there on the porch with me if he had had a choice. He would have held me close and kissed me and said he loved me more than anything, and we would have slow danced to the imaginary music that always seemed to play in our heads. Then we would have laughed for no reason and kissed again because that is just what we did . . . on any given day . . . at any given time. We laughed and kissed. My son called, and then my daughter and the group thought it was great that my grown children rang my cell phone at midnight to say "Happy New Year." None of their cell phones rang. Of course, my children know I am alone; they look after their momma.

On New Year's Day his prayer book tells me to live one day at a time in the new year. I resolve to follow those instructions. The past is over, and I cannot control tomorrow, so I will deal with today. My son calls and invites me to lunch. I go and enjoy the precious baby girl and their company. Next, I go to an open house and have a wonderful time visiting with friends I haven't seen in several weeks. The conversation is light and silly, and we share our laughter. We wish each other good health and good things for 2003. It is time to go to a movie with a friend to round out the day. By bedtime, I am able to believe that the holidays were good. Not spectacular like last year, but good. Shared. Soothing. Comforting. Bittersweet. Perfect word . . . bittersweet.

BREATHE   CREATE   SHARE   SING   REJOICE   CHERISH

Do not allow the first holiday season without your loved one to be a nightmare. Take control of the season before it begins. Announce that you have made a plan before you are dragged hither and yon by well-meaning family and friends. Under no circumstances are you to buy into the idea that "everything must be exactly as it always has been for the sake of the children, the family," etc. Keep some or most of the things you have always done, but try something new. Perhaps you can start a small, new tradition. Go caroling, take a carriage ride, visit outlying towns, change some of your tree ornaments, leave your home and visit family and friends in their homes. They will understand the need for a change if you explain in advance. But try not to "dump" old friends because you think the memory will be painful. Include them in your plans. What will you do?

The important thing is to stay busy every day of the holidays. "Busy" includes planned relaxation and visiting, or reading, and seeing movies. Visit new places. Don't decide to spend the holiday season cleaning a closet, or cutting yourself cut off from everyone because you are mourning. Good mourning includes good living; it includes sharing your laughter with good friends, enjoying the company of people, and extending yourself to others less fortunate. Cook a good meal and send it to a family in need. When you open your arms to others, what you give comes back.

What is your holiday plan?

Any New Year's resolutions? Resolve to make none. For the coming year, live only one day at a time. Deliberately.

*   *   *

MONTH SIX

SIX MONTHS

It is Sunday, January 5, 2003, the first Sunday of the new year. I am totally irrational and illogical. I rose at 8:00 a.m., took a half-way disinterested look at the paper (I can't focus on anything today), dressed, drove to church and sang with the choir. I walked around the corner and bought flowers and went to the cemetery and put them on his grave. And stupid thoughts keep running through my head. A running conversation among God, him, and me . . .

"Well, . . . six months and I'm here. Where the hell are you?

You have a grave for people to visit. I have no grave and no one with whom to be buried. Divorce does that I guess. Breaks up families so mom is here, dad is there . . . of course, the ex never wanted to be buried . . . he will be given to science, and he never really bothered about what would happen to me or where I would be put. Perhaps I should be cremated and scattered to the winds since I really belong with no one. You're with your dead wife. And when we discussed it, you said when we married you would consider getting a plot with me, but yours was paid for and you hated to waste money on getting a new one. "Don't spend money on death," you said. We would discuss it in the future we decided, but the future never came for us did it? We only had Now. You know, sometimes Now is not enough.

I feel like saying every curse word I can think of, but what good would that do? You'll still be dead, and I'll still be alone. This is a bad weekend. Yesterday was the ex's birthday; today you are gone six months. The man who did not love me is alive and well; the man who loved me is dead and gone. I'm screwed and alone either way.

In church I thought of the irony: I'm a practicing Catholic, married for life. I got left; you came into my life, devout and spiritual and a practicing Catholic, but we can't get married because my life is being held in the balance awaiting an annulment. My life is on hold because someone left me . . . I didn't leave him . . . but I'm the one in jeopardy. Fascinating. And now I am alone again.

You know, you were not alone very long. Friends surrounded you . . . kids . . . then you came to my door. You said you had mourned your wife for the two years that she was dying and she wanted you to find someone immediately. At six months you had me waiting at home for you after you went to the cemetery. There's nobody waiting for me, and there probably will never be. Today, I've lost all that confidence you built up in me; all that emotional strength you gave me is gone today. I'm back feeling the way I often felt over the years . . . not quite lovable . . . cold . . . ice queen. You really were lucky. I mean when your wife died, she sent you to my door because she was afraid for you to be alone. Well, are you sending someone to my door? You know I don't do the dating routine. We had history and friendship to bring us together. Common ground.

All of that is gone. I wasn't planning on being loved by you. It was a wonderful, happy accident, and today I'm sorry you ever came to my door.

Six months without seeing you

Twenty-six weeks of going places without you

One hundred-eighty days of not talking to you

Four thousand three hundred twenty hours of not feeling your presence

Two hundred fifty-nine thousand two hundred minutes of having just enough oxygen to stay alive for not much reason.

God blessed you. You had me with you. You died just the way you wanted, and I was there as I had predicted. Remember when I told you that the day we were cutting grass? I said your wife's reward for loving you through the drinking years was not to have to bury you. And I said the price I would pay for loving you was that I would have to bury you. You kissed me and told me not to think of such things. I've paid a great price. I saw you out. Was with you when that last breath was taken. Watched the life go out of you. Kissed you until you were cool. Tried to save you, but I couldn't. Was there something else I could have done? Did you know you were having a heart attack? Would somebody just talk to me and give me some answers? I know we were good for each other. We were perfect in every way together. We adored each other. I know you would be with me if you had a choice today. But what happens to me now? See, I'm caught lying again. God always gets me. The one-day at a time lie I told on New Year's Day . . . I won't worry about the future, only take it one day at a time. If I were doing that, I wouldn't be in this awful mood . . . I would be taking down the Christmas tree and preparing to set the table for dinner with my children and the baby. Right? I would be getting on with it, getting things done. Right? So, I guess I need to stop moping and typing and get on with life. 'I got along without you before I met you . . . gonna get along without you now . . .' This would be easier if you had left me before you died . . . if you had gone away . . . it wouldn't be hurting now . . . it would be a quiet, perhaps indifferent feeling . . . not this emptiness . . . this lack . . . this unforgiving solitude that never fills. The other irony is that I know I am a widow but no one knows it . . . five weddings we went to in that one year, and at each one we said "I do."

It is ten p.m., again. I hate this time on Friday nights, and I hate this time tonight. I think they were telling me you were dead at this time. Or maybe I just knew in my heart that you were dead. Funny. I can't remember the exact time today for some reason.

My children came over and had lunch and threw away the Christmas tree. We all ceremoniously strolled the tiny angel, and I was relieved to have the company. Then they left, and I wrote thank you notes to students, spoke to a friend on the phone, and left to go to a friend's house. We had a lovely visit, and she gave me three rolls of pictures that were found at your house; our trips to Charleston and Cancun. It was like a Christmas gift for me. You and I look so happy in those pictures. And there is the one of you showing off your engagement ring. What a happy day that was! So sudden, so unexpected, so you! But it is ten o'clock, and all of that is gone. Gone with you. Six months. Jesus . . . it might as well be a thousand years."

BREATHE   SET GOALS   TRAVEL   DO UNTO OTHERS

Six months have passed. Does anger rise up in your chest every now and then like heartburn? Call a friend and vent, then go on to something else. Don't let anger ruin your attitude.

Have you found a hobby or new activity? It can be anything that ever appealed to you: a foreign language, music, meditation, yoga, exercise, Bible study, volunteer work. Anything that will take you out of your house and yourself is beneficial. What would you like to try?

We need things to look forward to. Plan a trip. It can be short and inexpensive or long and elaborate. Quick weekends of changing scenery can give a nice lift. Plan it. Do it. Where are you going?

It is extremely important to do things for other people. This keeps us connected to the living and the moment. If you have relatives and children or grandchildren, they can occupy your time. But check the needs list at a local church. See what they need and what you can do. Don't depend entirely on your family to be your life. It's not totally fair to them. It cheers them up when you call and say you are going out with friends; it says you are coming back to life.

MENDING THE PIECES

It's time to tape your photo back together. Line up the numbers in order and tape very neatly. Now turn the photo over. Fix any messy spots by re-taping carefully. Now look at yourself. Yes, you are a bit scarred here and there, but you are still here piecing yourself back together. It's been six months.

Read the back of the photo. Are your words and thoughts improving? Regressing? Remaining static? It's okay. This becomes a progress report of sorts. If you are regressing into fear, constant anger, and daily depression, you should seek professional counseling immediately. Time is passing, and if you are locked in a place that is not good, you won't heal.

If your words all seem to express the same mood, try to start the next month with something new. On blocks 27-30 of your photo write one thing you want to do; one thing you want to stop doing; one thing you want to keep; one thing you want to lose (it can be abstract, like an emotion).

Why did you choose those four things?

THE SECOND SIX MONTHS

MONTH SEVEN

A CALM SILENCE

It is mid January and I have been away from my writing. I don't know why really. I read his prayer book and meditations every night, and he is the last thought I have before I sleep. I think of him often, but it is not in a sad way. It's almost as though he has become a power source for me. I feel his presence around me, and I cannot be sad. I just feel so secure; it's like he's standing behind me with his arms wrapped around me. What happened to me Sunday is typical and will illustrate what I mean.

One of my students won a prize in an essay competition. Five hundred entries, really big prize for her, her teacher, and the school. I was told that one of my students had won one of the big prizes. I was standing there thinking that he and I had gone to the ball park last year together for this same contest's ceremony, and we had had such fun at the ball game. Third place was called and the winner went forward; then they began to read the second place winner. It wasn't my student, so I knew she had gotten first place. In the split second I realized it, I felt him throw his arms around me from the back. It was so real that I actually bent my head and put my arms on my stomach to touch his hands there. It all happens in one small, swift motion that no one notices. He is just so "here." I can't explain it, but it makes me feel wonderful. Yes, I do miss his physical presence, but I think I'm taking on his essence. I think I'm gaining his wisdom. I find words coming out of my mouth that people say, "Oh, that's a great idea . . . the perfect thing to say . . ." and I don't know where they come from. Maybe it's the Holy Spirit at work in me. But there is a silence that falls after all the holiday activities. I hated it at first, now I am in it and I keep moving through it. I play his blues music he bought the day he died and never got to hear. The first song on the CD, "Stormy Monday" is one he used to sing to me. It was like getting a gift from him when it started. I just sat down on the sofa and listened. I laughed and sang along because suddenly we were under a tree in Memphis where an old blues man was playing the same song. What a great trip that was! But that's another story.

SEVEN MONTHS

What are you trying to tell me today? All day I've had your face right in front of me. We've finished dinner, and you are grateful for another simple yet elegant meal for two. You show your gratitude with that precious smile. And you keep looking right into my eyes. The way you always do. Soul lock. Looking into my most secret places. Saying thousands of words without speaking. Wait. I have to touch your dimple. Kiss it. Trace the lines on your face with my fingers. Memorize your nose and mouth. The crow's feet you earned from squinting in the glare off your boat. Have I told you today how I adore you? How when I hold your hand I'm energized? How I think nothing is impossible because you love me? Have I told you today? Is this what you want me to write about? I felt you draped around me all day. What's today? Why is it special? It's just like any of our other days. Incredibly charged. Giddy. Thoughtful. Full of intelligent conversation. You know what I love about our conversations? I love their scope. I mean we talk about everything imaginable in a few hours. W.E.B. Griffith has a new book out. I know you'd already have finished it, Speedreader. I love how you devour books and how you enjoy watching me linger over the words, sucking thought juice out of phrases.

Coffee? Fully leaded or caffeine-free? Why do I ask? It's always fully leaded. What is today's message? God . . . I feel you in the room here. I just wrapped my arms around you. I love to hug you that way when you're sitting there at the dinner table with me.

I went to the race track Sunday, and I haven't been the same since. I was just so separate from the group. You and I had talked so often about getting a table together to go for dinner and the races, but it didn't work out. So there I was driving into the parking lot alone. And of course I remembered Jazz Fest, the last time we had been there. We sat in the club house and listened to Elvis's guitar player talk; then Aaron Neville in the Gospel Tent, and you took pictures of me while I played the tambourine with the Mardi Gras Indians. And you touched my neck when we sat under a shade tree to wait for the Neville Brothers. Usually I can get on with it, but this time I'm feeling stuck.

Tomorrow is seven months. I've had dinner and taken a walk. I've looked at the moon and the stars. I know if I look hard enough I'll see your face, but I can't quite find it. Like I'm trying to find a strand of hair that occasionally rolls in front of my eyes then escapes my grasp. Seven months. I seem to be losing my focus. I have no idea of the future anymore, and it seems to be dragging me down. I have to stay in the moment. I think I've misplaced that the last few days. Think of nothing but this moment. Then the past and the future offer no problems. For this moment I am talking to you because I am desperate for our conversations. We would have had so much to say to each other over the events of the week. The Columbia space shuttle crew is gone. They have been cut into stars and placed next to you. And you "shall make the heavens so bright that everyone will fall in love with night and pay no worship to the garish sun." How did Shakespeare know that?

I'm typing in front of your picture. You have your arm around me as always, pulling me close. You are looking directly into the camera with that look that I love on your face. I miss you so terribly tonight. It's not painful like it was at first. Now it's an emptiness. Pain was something. Emptiness is nothing. Seven months and I feel as if I'm taking the first steps on a journey across dry sand. No waves. No sea breeze. Just dry sand.

BREATHE   PRAY   STAY IN THE MOMENT   EXTEND LOVE

Yes, it will get better, but you will have down times. Angry times. Vacant times. They are tiring aren't they? Try to keep your faith in today.

In this second six months you will feel more alone because friends go on with life because they see you getting along well. Six months seems to be a cut-off point for people who have not suffered this kind of loss. They can't understand it because they haven't experienced it. Be patient with them, but don't harp on them or turn your anger on them. They can't help it that they don't quite get it.

It's time for you to share you insights with others who have suffered your loss. Take what you have learned and apply it to their experience. Let them cry on you, vent on you, hug you. Comfort them. You are becoming an expert at salving the savage wounds that you have already survived. Pull these people along. Besides just being there for them, what can you tell them? How can they get from one day to the next? They will want some word from you because your experience has made you trustworthy.

This is the month when you feel like caving in. Stay in the moment. "Nothing is more important than this day." Repeat Goethe's words aloud a few times. Hang them on a mirror.

MONTH EIGHT

NEW YORK THEN AND NOW

The e-mail was waiting at my Singapore hotel.

"I know we said we wanted to go to New York sometime, so I have made all the arrangements for September 21, 22, 23, 2001. I have tickets for the top of the Empire State Building. We will make a wish. I love you." I replied:

"I insist on taking you to see *Phantom of the Opera*. Get tickets for me. Can't believe I've done Hong Kong, Bangkok, Chaing Mai, and now Singapore without you. I will have stories to occupy you for months. I wonder if I am the same since I have seen this side of the world. Surely I have grown to love you more in my absence."

And so we went to New York. It was a surreal experience. The city had been bombed by terrorists on the eleventh, and we had the streets to ourselves. Merchants were delighted to see us; restaurants welcomed us, but everywhere we went, we became therapists. New Yorkers wanted to know how everyone felt about them around the country. They began to tell of lost friends and neighbors. Oddly, in that city that never stops moving we found people throwing their arms around us, wanting to sit and talk, thanking us for listening, thanking us for coming, thanking us for not letting terrorists dictate our lives.

It was the first weekend of autumn, and a carriage ride through Central Park made us believe we owned the whole piece of property. So few people were enjoying the beautiful day. In a city of millions, there was a sense of small town America, of connectedness; everyone seemed to have lost someone, and needed comfort. We strolled an absolutely silent Greenwich Village on Saturday. We spent an hour in a music shop specializing in old jazz, rhythm and blues, and rock and roll. He purchased a copy of the original "Soldier Boy" by the Four Fellows. The owner found it in the basement of his store that was only about eight feet wide. The owner was foreign-born and had very little to say. We were evidently friendly enough that he finally smiled and thanked us for coming by and said it was a pleasure to talk to someone who knew so much about music. As we left the shop, a woman with a stroller came toward us. We smiled. She smiled. I told her I was visiting and she started to talk quietly of her fifteen neighbors who had died. All firemen. All her friends. All fathers with children in this neighborhood. She asked us to go to the corner with her. There, we were greeted with that unforgettable sight of pictures of the missing hanging on the fences, and across the street not one but two fire stations strewn with flowers and photographs of the dead. She put her arms around us and we stood together like family. We didn't ask her name. It didn't seem necessary to know names. We just knew that we were family, and we had all been marked by this terrible loss.

The end of the Island was off limits, but the air was acrid and dusty and there was a certain bit of anger in the atmosphere. In China Town there was no hustle or bustle, and in Little Italy no one argued over pasta. A very different New York than I had seen the first time.

Ironically, we had a marvelous time because we had every tourist attraction to ourselves, and we were the center of everyone's attention. But we devoted our attention to the city. It is such a marvelous place. Hong Kong is her replica only larger; built by money for money. Manhatten lay before us like a wounded giant licking a severe but not deadly wound. In the distance one could imagine a roar of the thing willing itself back to full strength. A different New York.

The Theatre District was open, but the audiences were sparse. As curtain time approached, people filed in quietly. There was a pall over everything, and this was my very favorite play. I hoped the cast was up for the performance. The overture began. Nothing had changed. An incredibly solid troupe of professionals giving their all, and I wondered how many of them had lost friends. The music seemed to wipe all the tragedy away. We were magically transported, and the constant pulsating rhythm of the music lifted everyone to some other place. When the curtain fell the audience rose as one body and applauded. But there were no "bravos" or yells or whistles; only constant, solid, hard applause. An audience in mourning. A different New York.

The Empire State Building was off limits, and he was disappointed because he said it would be the perfect romantic thing to do. He wanted to buy roses and toss the petals down. We promised each other we would return the next year. I bought a card with a drawing of the building on it and wrote a note: "Hold the thought, my love. We'll be there in twelve months."

It is seventeen months later, and I am returning to that city. I will revisit things I have seen, and I will see new things. I will be with family and friends, and I will keep the promise and go the top of the Empire State Building. Only I will carry with me fourteen dried roses from his coffin. One for each month we shared. I am not at all sure I can strew the air with the petals. I am not sure I can let them go. But I will try. I must move forward as he did. It will be a different New York. A different me.

ELLIS ISLAND TO GROUND ZERO, 3/3/03

So many emotions in one day. Our bus tour began with a six below zero wind-chill in the air, and we took the downtown loop. I had seen all this last year, and it was a comfort to relive the moments I had shared with him. But when we were here, the loop ended at the Village because of the bombing. It was the smell, an acrid, chemical dusty odor, that day that told us something was amiss; it was the quiet; it was the smoky cloud hanging over the end of the island.

Today, it was the hole that screamed at me. For blocks we drove down the street and saw daylight on our right. Blocks of daylight. Blocks where the towers had stood. We did not stop; we went to Battery Park and lined up for the ferry. The cold was so deep our skin burned, but we had a constant and brilliant view of the harbor. We boarded. I found myself filling up with emotion as I thought of my in-laws. He had arrived at Ellis Island as a teen; she, seeing the Statue on the Fourth of July, 1946, from the deck of a ship.

In the sun the Lady shone as brilliantly as usual, and the shutters of cameras clicked incessantly. We entered the museum at Ellis Island. It has been restored to exactly what it was in the days of immigration. It was as emotional as the Holocaust Museum in Washington, but for the opposite reason: life, liberty, pursuit.

"My mother put me on the boat and told me to make a life in America. I never saw her again."

"I came to America alone because we had money for only one fare. I was a fourteen year old boy. Everything I had was in a straw basket."

"I may be barefoot, but I will be barefoot in America."

"I will sweep streets if I have to, but I will be sweeping in America."

Ironically, from nearly every window the blank spot could be seen in the distance: the New York skyline minus something. Some being from another planet would never know the difference in the skyline. But the ghosts of these immigrants know. It is an emotion-filled place, this Ellis Island. And finally, a red sign hanging overhead reminded the immigrant newcomers: "Be loyal"; and through the window just below the sign, the blank space in the city skyline.

Back on the ferry a cacophony of accents and languages gave me the feeling it could be any day when Ellis Island was in full operation. Off the ferry, I walked with a mission, my face wrapped against the wind. I was going to see what we could not see together a year ago. I was going to pay respects for both of us to the dead. Walk, turn. Observe. Attend.

At the corners of Church and Liberty Streets. The blank spot. The vast twenty-two acres where seven buildings are missing. A vast pit. An uncommon communal crematorium. I began to whisper "mercy." If I could say it three thousand times perhaps I could do my part to fill the hole. But I could not say it fast enough. Three thousand souls robbed of their right to die peacefully. Three thousand souls robbed of the right to say good-bye. Three thousand souls robbed of the chance to say a final prayer for mercy. "Mercy" I said aloud, and I wept. I wept for them and their families. I wept the tears I knew he would have cried with me. Angry tears for innocents lost. The longing for him was so powerful at that moment that I had to hold on to the fencing for fear that I would sink to the sidewalk and become hysterical. The mercy I asked for was not only for those lost in the pit.

I walked the length of the block and turned the corner. A cordoned off area was ahead. Several people stood inside weeping. This is a viewing area for the families of victims. I told the officer I had come to pay my respects and he added my city to his list of the day. He looked at me and saw I had been crying. He put his arm around me. "Now promise me you won't cry anymore. We can't let them stop us. We're building it again. This is New York. We're building it up again."

I crossed the street to St. Paul's Church, the building from 1760 miraculously undisturbed by the mega-collapse at its door. On a table a sign: "This was the supply table where firemen came for new boots as theirs melted in the 2,000 degree heat of the debris piles." Two thousand-degree debris pile; digging for bones and body parts. Back across the street at the hole, a banner under a twisted cross-shaped girder reads "Never Forget." The names of all the dead are printed on signs on the fencing. It is breathtaking in its awfulness. The wind picks up. It whistles and whispers over the vast pit. The words of those immigrants on Ellis Island ring in my ears : "America is hope . . . America is life." Mercy, Lord. Mercy.

NEW YORK REPRISE

Let me preface this by saying I believe in those people who receive messages from people who have crossed over. I have come to believe that those who have left this earth are still active in a good and happy place. I say this because of the things that have happened to me in the last eight months. I read a book that said the dead speak to us in symbols, that they are with us on special occasions, and that they can continue to guide us if we listen or look at the symbols. I was very skeptical about all of this at first, but I have had so many messages from the man who loved me that I have begun to feel like the woman in that wonderful movie *The Ghost and Mrs. Muir*. Anyway, I have returned from New York, and I have several reasons why I know he took the trip with me.

First, I am terrified of flying and he removed that fear. I was hesitant about the flight without him, but I could feel him holding my hand, and I was fine. On our trip to New York we had gone to dinner and one of the songs played was "As Time Goes By," his favorite. This time, I was with family, and we went to dinner and were seated. We were chatting and the music started: "As Time Goes By." Welcome to New York, honey.

A native told us if we had free time one evening to see a movie in a high rise on Times Square. I had managed to miss *Adaptation* in New Orleans, so that was the choice. *Casablanca* was always our favorite film, and we watched it a few times together. So here I am in the show and one of the characters starts going on about how *Casablanca* is the best screenplay ever written. My message from him for the day.

But it was at Ground Zero that he made his presence felt. We were in New York on September 22, 2001, but the area was locked down. On this visit as I reached the center of the block, hanging on the fence were two huge aerial photographs. One was dated September 11, 2001. Next to it, the other was dated September 22, 2001. I smiled. Had to be him giving me a message. Why would a photo be taken on that date? Not a week, or thirty days or three months, or six months or a year. Eleven days? Everyone found that a bit odd. I found it to be a message in a bottle, set sail on the cosmos.

Finally, I kept my promise and went to the top of the Empire State Building with rose petals. I was going to do what he had wanted to do: throw them over New York. In the lobby I decided I couldn't go through with it. My daughter told me I had to have this fun for him. I thought this might be the one thing I could not do. I proceeded. The wind was gusty at times, and my head was wrapped in a scarf against the cold. In sight of the Chrysler Building, his architectural favorite, I tossed the petals. They hung before me in the air current for a few seconds, as though he wanted a last chance to dance with me or kiss my cheek; then, they were whipped up and away. Some came to rest on the decorative concrete ornament next to me. My daughter and I watched them. They would not go. She and I gasped through our tears. We watched as we held on to each other, and we blew them into the night sky. We ducked inside away from the cold and I pretended to examine items in the gift shop, but really I was trying to regain my composure. I had kept the promise to go to the top. Some promises are nearly too painful to keep. We began our trek back to our hotel. No cabs were available so we walked thirteen blocks bundled against the chill.

That night we had to pack for a dawn airport trip. I was relieved that my hair did not need washing or setting. I bathed, packed and slept. In the morning I began to comb my hair. There in the back of my hair, stuck together, were two rose petals from the night before when my head had been covered by a scarf. A thank you to me for going back to New York? A way of letting me know he was there? Something to comfort me for the pain of the night before. I put the petals in his prayer book that I read daily, more convinced than ever that he is still very near.

BREATHE   PLAN   PRAY   GO

Did you make a promise to your loved one, or did you have a special trip or plan that you dreamed of doing together? Plan it and do it. If it was a huge trip that may be impossible now, scale it down and do something you know the person would have enjoyed. What will it be?

Changing space, even briefly, gives a new perspective. Go someplace you want to see. Observe the surroundings. What did you see, hear, smell? Did you speak to anyone? What did you discuss?

MONTH NINE

PALM SUNDAY—OF PETS AND BABIES

T.S. Eliot was right when he said that April is the cruelest month. It is the beauty of the days that is so disturbing to those of us who have fond memories of past Aprils. My grandmother died in April as did my father. But those events do not sadden me. She was very old, and he was ready to die. It is the memories of the two past Aprils that are suffocating me today. April 2001 brought me the love of my life; April 2002 saw that love full blown and profound. April, 2003 offers the pain of what might have been. Had he been here today, we would have gone to mass and walked to the French Quarter Festival and danced in the street and talked to people we knew and people we had never seen before. I know this because last year we saw his nephew who said to us, "I hope we're as cool as you two are when we're your age." I hope they will be. So, today I went to church for the beginning of Holy Week services. Funny how the words to some antiphons bring on the tears. On the third go around of "My God, my God, why have you abandoned me?" I sang as the tears rolled. And I wasn't really thinking of anything in particular. And Jazz Fest begins in two weeks and we would have been there together. So April is indeed cruel in New Orleans. It and October have always been my favorite months in this city on the river. In our April and October we shared more than some do in years, and my memories are perfect, but they are memories. I need some tangible warmth. Is it time for a dog?

I've noticed that people who live alone have pets. It does my heart good to see my grand dog Hector. He is a lovable, laughable golden retriever that throws himself on me and licks my feet until I giggle. I'm ticklish. I must say that I have been so lonesome that I have been contemplating a dog, or perhaps a cat. Since I had a cat, I know they are independent and easier to board when I travel than a dog. The idea of either one sounds great when I'm down, but reality sets in and I remember the responsibility. Do I want that? My answer came at lunch today.

After mass I was so down I phoned my son to see what they were doing and told him I'd like to see the baby today. He said they were on the way to lunch and I should join them. Now we've all got that urge to squeeze babies (especially our own grandbabies). However, my grandbaby is very attached to her momma because Momma is the only food source allowed. I have joked with friends that I am not allowed closer than three feet to her because she cries if Momma gets out of sight. So after being patient for nearly six months, I was rewarded today. She sat on my lap in the restaurant and was perfectly content. This was really a gift to me. It made my whole day. I think she has gotten used to the idea that I'm someone who sees her several times a week, and that I love her. It was all warm and fuzzy. Can't wait to feed her some baby food. Most baby food smells better that wet cat food or dog food. Add that plus to the list of pros and cons, and I have made a decision. I'll make the baby my pet. Make her rotten; send her home. And the day ends, if not on a great high note, at least with a contented smile.

SINGING IN HOLY WEEK

I will admit that I have spent the Easter holiday in hiding. But I chose to hide in church and sing with the choir for the services. I puttered during the day and sang every night. I guess we are often drawn to what we need without even knowing it. For once, I listened to all the words of the various services, and they became very soothing to my psyche. Of course, I could relate to the story and how it all related to my life.

There was Naomi who said "the Almighty has dealt bitterly with me." There was Jesus who made the comments "one whom I have cherished has betrayed me." "This day thou shalt be with me in paradise." "My God, why have you abandoned me?" "Into your hands I commend my soul." By the time I got to that line, I was able to paraphrase a few things: He is with God in paradise; into God's hands I have commended his soul, and finally, on Easter Sunday, "He is not here. He is risen."

On Good Friday I visited the cemetery and had a chat with the man who loved me. He always said his dead wife sent me to take care of him. So I made an Easter request. I asked for him to send me a life. Not necessarily a person, but a life. If it is to be a person, I guess I could handle that. But I need some plan or purpose as I begin again. His first gift was a beautiful Easter.

Last Easter we had the two families together at his home for the day. It was exciting and hectic and fun. This year my family gathered with me for dinner at my home. We were ten, and the angel baby was the center of my attention. She is so beautiful that I don't know whether to smile or cry when I look at her. He told me many times I would love being a grandmother. And he is right, but I wish he were here to share my joy. My day began with singing a Mozart mass with the philharmonic at St. Patrick's Church. It occurred to me that I have sung for people from across the world as tourists pack the church on Sundays. We had an inspired morning and it was a gorgeous sound. At the end of mass the congregation remained and gave us a standing ovation. Of course, we ended with the Hallelujah Chorus with the organist rattling the roof and the bells peeling. This crowd had to have been convinced that Christ had indeed risen. The rest of the day was smooth and peaceful and so pleasant. When everyone left at six, I was content to relax and rest. There was no depressed feeling when they left as there had been on every other occasion since he died. I think he listened Friday and is getting to work. Time will tell.

APRIL DREAMS

In dreams he still comes to me. When I awake I have little or no memory of what I dreamed, but I know he was there. It is usually a physical presence I feel. We are just together in a room or a car or on a street. Last night, Easter Sunday night, we were riding in his car and I was holding his hand. I remember pressing my two hands together over his to make sure he was real. I held his hand up and put mine on either side and pressed. I couldn't make my hands touch so we laughed. I said, "I just wanted to make sure I wasn't dreaming." He answered, "No, I'm here. I'm real." It was so wonderful, and I felt comforted when I awoke.

BREATHE　　　CREATE　　　LAUGH　　　EMBRACE　　　HELP

Get a living thing. A green plant; a pet. Spring brings new energy. If necessary, force yourself outside to soak up daylight and sun; smell the air.

Get out and do the events your town offers. Listen to the music of the streets; go to festivals; eat ice cream; laugh.

Keep doing small things for other people. This will become very rewarding to you. Remembering people in prayer or meditation is a gift. Let them know that you pray for them or think of them. Who have you prayed for lately?

TEN MONTHS

TEN MONTHS

I went to mass at St. Jude's Church and the piano playing made me weep. It was my first time back there since he died, and we went so often together that being alone made me nearly hysterical. I managed to control myself until I got in the car, and then I was able to weep and wail as I drove. This does not get easier as time passes. I just feel less whole each day. I guess I am failing him because his mission was to complete me. He did, but then he died, and I am no longer whole.

I go through the motions of being okay with everything. I see people, I teach, I love my grandbaby, but there is a void that I was hoping I could fill, and I just can't. I guess nothing will ever be the same, but we go through the motions and hope that one day it will be better.

I went out last night on a group date. Two couples and a single gentleman and myself. It was a lovely evening of theatre and chat, but that was all. Ten months. A thousand years. Same difference.

That was May 5. Today is May 10. It has been two years since the fish dinner we cooked and ate. Two years since the hug and kiss that changed my life. And in the two years an incredible fourteen months that made me a different person. Then ten months of a vacancy I cannot fill.

I have learned what causes addictions. It is an unfillable vacancy. Some people fill the hole with food, others with liquor, others with drugs. I fill it with motion. Perhaps that is the least destructive.

I finished directing the last play of the year, and it seems what I have lost in companionship I have made up for in inspiration. I just wish I could have a conversation with it and get an answer. Hold its hand. Hug it. Two years since our love began. How time flies. Tomorrow is Mother's Day, and I will smile and wallow in my wonderful children—all four—and rejoice in my grandbaby. And I will try desperately to fill the space.

BREATHE WORK VISIT PHONE PRAY CREATE ACCEPT

Are you piecing together your second photograph? Are your weekly words sounding better? If not, get help. If so, time is healing your wound.

How is your health? Have you been back to the doctor? Are you eating well? Walking? Sleeping well? Taking vitamins? Relaxing?

Stay in touch with other people. Call someone you haven't spoken to in a while. Be a good listener. Have some friends over and create a meal for them, or write a poem, draw, or sing a song just for yourself. Just let your creative juices flow in some way.

MONTH ELEVEN

ELEVEN MONTHS

The grace of God is a wonderful gift. Two years ago today on June 6, 2001, we went to the D-Day Museum in New Orleans and ate lunch at a local hole in the wall, Juan's Flying Burrito. He was amazed that I was so bohemian in my choice of eateries. We strolled Magazine Street's wonderful shops and had a great day. The following June found us on a big summer trip up the East Coast to Boston, Philadelphia, Washington and Connecticut. An incredible trip that was enjoyable every moment, and punctuated with discussions of our wedding plans.

This June I am alone, and it has been eleven months since his death. Yesterday was a beautiful day for me. I took my daughter-in-law and granddaughter shopping. That may sound mundane, but it is the tiny normal things that have made these months bearable. I met a dear friend for lunch, and we spent the afternoon and early evening strolling the French Quarter. What fascinated me was my feeling of acceptance and, oddly, happiness. Time and prayer have ways of healing us.

In the first weeks and months I could only see his dying when I thought of him. I hid his pictures because they were too painful to see. Yesterday, as I drove alone from place to place, scenes of his last day kept popping up before me, and they were so wonderful that I could only feel good. We had such a good time doing things that day. We began with incredible conversation about the daily news, then we joined my cousins for brunch. We left them and drove to see my niece's home, and he talked to them as if they had known each other forever.

"Are you serious about him?" my niece asked me.

"Oh, yes. He wants to get married right now, but we have to wait for an annulment."

"Well, I think he's great, and I can tell he's crazy about you," she said.

She proceeded to show me her scars from recent plastic surgery for a tummy tuck after four babies.

When we left, I was telling him about her surgery and said I needed a tummy tuck. "You're a beautiful woman. I love you just like you are." was his reply. It was just a quiet comment. It was a statement with no "I think" in front of it. But that was how he loved me. It was very definite. There were never any statements that came in a compound sentence that began "I love you, but . . ." We loved each other absolutely and proved that Shakespeare was right: true love sees with the mind, not with the eye. And he is gone, but the knowledge that he loved me so completely in every way is all I can feel now.

To say I don't miss him would be untrue. There is a vacancy in me that I can never fill, but there is no unhappiness or bitterness. Unhappiness and bitterness would deny what we had. We loved so fully and completely and with such faith, that to be sad would be to appear ungrateful for the gift I was given. I was loved so completely in every way, spiritually, emotionally, intellectually, physically, that it is not possible to be sad. It was the most incredible and perfect thing that has ever happened to me besides the lives of my two children. I find that I can only be grateful.

These eleven months I have relied on the army of friends who saw me through the days one at a time. I learned this lesson when a Jewish friend's husband died quite suddenly. It is the Jewish tradition to mourn for eleven months. At the eleventh month the headstone is placed on the grave, and the widow is expected to get on with her life. I adapted that strategy, and I am feeling focused and I am getting on with things. Prayer has sustained me, along with just talking to his spirit when I have felt like it. Yes, I miss him awfully, but I can only rejoice that I had him in my life. He made me a woman in full, and I made his last year serene and secure and peaceful. He died a happy death, and I have the eternal memory of knowing his last words: "I love you more than you will ever realize. I love you more than you or anybody can ever understand." When those are the last words you hear from the person you have loved, those words can get you through the whole ordeal of mourning. They are like a vehicle driving you through uncharted territory. You may have no idea where you are headed, but you can rest in the backseat of your mind and let those words have the steerage of your course. That is God's grace at work, controlling the vehicle after we give up the wheel. It is acceptance of what we cannot change.

FLORIDA: ON THE ROAD AT FIFTY WEEKS

Two weeks short of a year since his death, I left for Florida with a dear friend. In the quiet car as she napped, the spirit of the man who loved me was suddenly present as we drove the road he and I had driven often together. It was a cloudy then rainy day, and his presence was so strong that I actually moved on the seat once because I could feel his hand on my knee. I mentioned this to no one. It was not sad, just comforting.

Two nights later my daughter called and began to cry telling me how she misses him. I told her to talk to him because he is with us and takes care of us. She seemed consoled. I enjoyed Naples, and one evening my friend's son suggested a good place to eat. Bucca di Beppo. I laughed because we had eaten at Bucca di Beppo in Austin. It was great fun. Sicilian food served family style with everyone at the table sharing the portions.

It amazes me that he sends me all these messages. I love it. It's like having his arm around me. The messages didn't end with the restaurant choice. In Ft. Meyers, we toured the Edison-Ford Museum, and when I walked into the gift shop, *Phantom of the Opera* was playing. One of his favorite songs. Then in Sarasota I looked over the bay and thought how he would have loved the view. We toured the Ringling Museum and when I entered the gift shop, *Phantom* was playing. Different city, same song. When I arrived home I was looking for local news and surfed onto a channel where a man was discussing how the deceased use music to communicate with the living. Took my breath away.

Today is June 26. A year ago we were planning our trip to Texas. This year I am planning my trip to San Francisco, one he had looked forward to. I became a bit glum as the afternoon wore on, and I went to the grocery. I decided to stop for a yogurt that would be my dinner. I walked into the shop and the flavors were on a magnet board. The customer ahead of me asked about them. The waitress said, "We have one more." She added another magnet: strawberry. Our favorite flavor. A chill went down my spine. People would probably think I've gone balmy, so I don't mention these things very often, but I know they are his way of telling me he is with me.

I am preparing a speech for my nephew's wedding in San Francisco. I keep busy, and I am spending more and more time with my grandbaby, but there is that vacancy. It is not quite a sadness. It is a lost piece of a beautiful jigsaw puzzle. The picture is grand, but there is a small hole at the center. Something missing.

BREATHE   ACCEPT   REMEMBER   SMILE   MOVE ON

Where are you on this journey? Do you believe you are improving? In what ways?

Have you found some sort of contentment? What makes you feel content? Have you counted your blessings lately? List some of them here. Count those blessings often; they reaffirm that you are progressing. Enjoy life one day at a time. Taste it; smell it; feel it. Moment by moment.

ONE YEAR

JULY 3

It is 3:00 AM, and I have been taken over by a feeling of dread. I have been busy devoting time to my grandbaby, and I wrote the speech for my nephew's wedding. I have been trying to believe I want to go to San Francisco, but I just don't. I think it's the timing.

In my mind tonight I am tied to a chair in an empty room while being forced to watch a clock attached to a time bomb. When the clock reaches July 5, 10:00 PM, it will go off in my face. Tied to the chair, I can do nothing to stop it. It's a terrible feeling of doom. I know I have to put my trust in God, and I have asked Him several times through the night to make me calm, but He must be busy somewhere else.

I'm being picked up in three hours for the airport, so I think I should give up on sleeping. I guess what's got me tonight is the fact that we had looked forward to this trip together. Going to the wedding in San Francisco, then on to Seattle, then into Canada. Big trip. And I am transferring my dread of having lost him to losing my children in accidents. And the terror of flying is back. He had taken that fear away. It's back in triple tonight. The devil must be at work overtime.

I am afraid I will appear to be a stick in the mud to the people at the wedding, and it's not very appropriate to be yammering on about my fiancé dying last year at this time. Puts a bummer on the party mood. So I will wear a smile. A mask. I will be pleasant and hopefully conversant on many subjects. I hope my depression does not shut down my memory for information. My daughter will be with me. I will appear brave for her sake. Chin up and all that. It's bull. You fake it till you make it.

BREATHE   KEEP MOVING   KEEP SMILING   PLAN

Don't you hate those moments when you doubt like the disciples in the storm at sea? I know that if I wait or pray, the calm will come. But we have those "moments." Just tell people, "I'm having a moment." Wipe your eyes or calm yourself and proceed. People with souls will understand.

How do you plan to spend the first anniversary of your loved one's death? Make it a day that person would have enjoyed. Plan it here. Don't let the day pass unmarked, and don't get talked into things you don't want to do. YOU plan the day.

THE 365TH DAY, JULY 5

I had planned the day in advance in my mind. I would be in San Francisco where we had planned to be together. I decided just what I would do. Being with family and friends for my nephew's wedding could have made the day difficult, but it went perfectly.

I had gone to San Francisco to speak at my nephew's wedding. First, there was the flight into Dallas then on to San Francisco. I had done this same route exactly two years before on my way to Singapore for my own son's wedding. That July there was a wonderful man waiting for me back in New Orleans. The following July he and I drove to Dallas, and I flew home alone to await the arrival of his body. This July was to be another happier occasion. I had written the speech carefully over a two-week period, and I quoted his philosophy in it. Actually, I think he may have been guiding the pen. I arrived on July 3 in time to walk the Union Square area and dress for the rehearsal dinner. It was good to have one of my dearest friends along, and my precious daughter, and my son-in-law. Dinner was lobster served in impeccable style overlooking the Pacific. It was spectacular in every way, and my sister and brother-in-law were, as usual, marvelous hosts.

July 4 arrived and with it that sense of dread that kept creeping into my brain. "July 5 is coming" the demon thoughts taunted. I was nervous about delivering the speech without being overcome by tears. The four of us did the tourist thing at Fisherman's Wharf and neighborhood and were not terribly impressed. I force myself to see these things so I can nod when other tourists discuss them.

By 2:00 my nerves were getting the better of me, and we cabbed back to the hotel and ate lunch at a neat little grill. In the middle of lunch I teared up and got the feeling I couldn't pull this off, but I had to do this for my sister. It was her son's day, and she had traveled to Singapore for my son. It was payback time. My friend bolstered my nerve.

I was having trouble controlling my shaking hands as the wedding neared. This is really unusual for me since I am used to speaking to groups. I stepped into a hallway and said in a low voice, "Come on, Angel, get me through this. I know you can." I took a deep breath and entered the room. I got the job done and it was a highlight of the event. The pressure was off. The evening was elegant with spectacular views of the city from atop the Bank of America Building. I had never been above fireworks on the Fourth of July, and it is quite a different sight to look down on them. I slipped out quietly at 10:30 while my daughter and other relatives partied on. My daughter said she would join me in the morning to spend the day with me.

The day began easily and we rested and left the hotel to do what I wanted. Four of us began to walk. We walked Chinatown on Grant Street and browsed the shops. At Old St. Mary's Church we stopped to offer a prayer for his soul, and I lit a candle and placed it in the Chapel of Remembrance there. When I left the church I stood in the street and began to cry. My daughter cried with me. We shared a hug and we began to laugh. "Hike on, girl. We are walking these hills," I said. We laughed again, and I suddenly felt a great relief. We trekked on and came to City Lights Bookstore. I laughed when I thought he would probably have wanted to punch somebody after reading the anti-American titles in the basement, but my son-in-law who does stand-up comedy took my love's place and did an impromptu routine on a book called *Why America's Soldier's Should Die.* I was laughing so hard I had to leave the room before we were both evicted. We continued our climb to Telegraph Hill and Coit Tower.

By now we were getting the giggles from the chill air and possible lack of oxygen. I learned quickly to lean into the hill, but when you are laughing you have a tendency to lean backward which could send you downhill on a fast tumble. We reached the top and saw the bridge shrouded in thick fog while the rest of the city was clear. I had one more thing to do.

After going to the top of the tower, I walked into the gift shop. A radio station was playing music and after some announcements more music began. I wasn't paying attention, and it suddenly registered. It was *Phantom of the Opera.* I touched my son-in-law's arm. "Do you hear that song?"

"It's *Phantom*. Why?"

"Just checking," I said. I wanted to make sure I was not mad. But it was my message. We stepped outside, I dug into my purse, and brought out a small plastic bag. My friend, my children, and I took more rose petals that I had saved from his funeral and let them go in the wind.

In the bright afternoon sun, a slip of moon was shining directly overhead. The moon we loved to watch and walk under, and I knew he was there smiling on the four of us. So I had strewn rose petals from Atlantic to Pacific in two cities he had loved, New York and San Francisco. I spread my fingers wide beneath the moon and the petals whipped away toward the sun. And pieces of my heart flew up to the heavens. Yet, there was a feeling of completion in me. As though I had set the headstone or raised a plaque to honor him. I had a terrible urge to weep until I caused a mudslide, but God sends quick messages and this one was "Smile for your daughter; she misses him so much." So I smiled through teary eyes. We set off down the hills taking silly pictures of ourselves on the insanely pitched streets. The more I walked, the better I felt. There was only one more thing I had planned for the day.

I had mentioned to the family that I was going to a special place for dinner on July 5th. We met in the hotel lobby and went to Bucca di Beppo to eat. He and I had eaten at a Bucca's in Austin and had a great time. There were nine of us including another nephew that I rarely get to see. Oddly enough, he had met my love. So everyone at the table knew the man who loved me, and we raised a toast to him and spent the rest of the evening eating good food and laughing and laughing till our faces hurt. Family and friends creating moments in a day he would have loved. It ended the year and marked his passing on a high note.

THIRTEEN MONTHS

THIRTEEN MONTHS AND BUNDLING

I have made a concerted effort to spend time cleaning, and it can be emotionally exhausting. Excavating actually. I began when my daughter-in-law and the baby left for Singapore. I was trying to stay busy so I wouldn't notice not seeing them. The following week my son left to join them for two weeks. I called Singapore to wish him happy birthday on July 23, and he said the baby was sick. It was just a small statement. Like a twig falling from a tree. But as I continued excavating, my twig became a bundle.

I went on to a drawer that contained all the brochures I had brought back from our last big trip up the East coast, June, 2002. I was going to patch them together and make it a gift to hang in his study. The negatives of the New York trip came next, and just seeing the words "New York" brought a smile to my face. There were years of thank you notes in a folder I had kept; students writing to say how I had touched their lives. Old textbooks came next; time to pitch. Photographs of me in several newspapers when I did the social and volunteer scene were on the shelves. I thought briefly of the people pictured there that I don't see anymore because when the marriage ended so did most of that. Made me wonder if a single woman has the same social value as a married one. Just little thoughts passing through the mind as the hands worked.

On July 24, my son's birthday, the morning paper arrived with a front page story on a former student of mine. He had been a star athlete and very well-known. He had died suddenly in his sleep of natural causes at the age of twenty-one. This was the first anniversary of his death."Unforgettable" was the title of the article, and it was so sad to read how his family is attempting to cope or not cope without him. I wanted so much to go to their home and say something to help them, but I did not. Sin of omission.

A folder of editorials by the columnist Leonard Pitts dating back over several years all discussed the loss of the value system the country used to espouse. No kidding. I needed to hear some music. The twigs of the week had become a bundle, and the bundle a boulder as I moved my large CD player to a new place in the room. I was suddenly Syphius pushing the rock up the hill, and I crumpled onto the floor in tears. It was all the little things, the good and bad memories, the happy and sad ones, the deeds undone, the desertions, the music. The load was too heavy to tote at that moment, but releasing it all in tears was helpful. The phone rang. I announced "If I had a bridge, I'd consider jumping."

"Not without me holding your hand," the faithful friend answered.

We laughed. I told her my tale of woe, and she listened. I told her I was upset with myself because intellectually I knew I had nothing to be down about, but I couldn't stop the blubbering. I showered. Water pounding on the top on my head always seems to improve my mood. Off to see a Shakespeare comedy with my friend. The evening ended with a sensational dinner party at another dear friend's home. Delicious food and exciting conversations in which we solved at least a third of the world's problems. Usually we solve half, but we were relaxing.

Today I rose and decided I needed to go to church. St. Jude's. I needed the music. I was not to be disappointed. We sang Malotte's "Our Father" and "I Surrender All." It was just what I needed. The music. That wonderful piano playing. The packed pews filled with faithful Christians who happen to be Catholic. Decent people. And I feel much better today after having found all the things that had been buried on shelves. I had no idea they would bundle up on me, but they did not crush me. I know I can move on. It is all part of beginning yet again.

BREATHE   BE   ENJOY   RE-CREATE YOURSELF

Have you pieced your photo back together? Read the words in the squares on the back. Jot some of them down here. If you have made the journey consciously, then you know you are wiser, stronger, simpler. You are still you. Only better.

ON BIRTHDAYS AND WISDOM

August 15 is one of those dog days of summer when people are rushing to get back from vacation, go on vacation, begin a school year, or send a kid off to college. It is a day for departures; the day that signals the last few days of summer. And in the South it is the date when everyone has had enough of sauna weather and wishes everyone else would just go away so clothes could be shed and cool showers enjoyed. My birthday.

Being the fourth child puts this birthday celebrating in perspective from earliest childhood. Especially when several members of the family are born in July and August. By the time the fifth or sixth cake is cut, the enthusiasm is wearing thin. Or the celebrations are lumped together, or cake is served in a restaurant on the road on vacation. At any rate I never felt that my birthday was that big a deal, and that was a direct result of subliminal childhood training. Then I got married.

I married a guy who was obviously not really big on celebrating birthdays. Compound this with the fact that our two children were born on July 24 and August 12, and it is easy to see how the 15th was a tired rerun. But I secretly harbored birthday fantasies.

I figured when I turned thirty-five there would be a huge party . . . Well, surely at forty the hubby would do a surprise bash. Instead I was asked the old standby question, "What do you want to do for your birthday?" This is where the Venus and Mars thing kicks in. Any woman knows that she's going to be asked that question, but never in a million years when she answers, "Oh, just something small and quiet," does she mean that. The Martian did small and quiet. Just us and the two kids at a neighborhood restaurant, but it was lovely actually because I was so delighted with my accumulated history at that point. On to fifty.

When I was forty-five I decided that on my fiftieth birthday I would plan and give myself a catered toga party on the deck that wrapped around our home. It would be Animal House without vomit or garbage cans of jungle juice. I made this decision because I was tired of friends having to plan my birthday celebrations. But that was five years away in some fantasy. When I turned forty-eight, the husband wasn't speaking to me; so that made the day special and relaxed for all of us. I think we ate cake and took Tums. Stress has a way of blocking memories. When I was forty-nine, he had moved out of the house, and I was mourning my brother who had died of cancer. When fifty came no one knew I had wanted a party. My home with the deck had been sold, and I was busy moving out. My daughter and I went to Boston and had a wonderful time. She was turning twenty-one and there we were, two women, remaking ourselves to fit the new mold life had cast for us, divorcee and adult child of a broken home. Close friends gave a formal tea for twenty at a downtown hotel. I felt I had become a participant in an accident everyone was watching but could not stop.

The first three fifties were spent in stolen time with friends as I spent most of the day every August 15th with my mother who loved me and was very old. But fifty-four was another story. It was the fantasy come to life.

After the trip of a lifetime, a tour of Asia culminating in the wedding of my son in Singapore, I returned home to a man who loved me. We had been friends for sixteen years, and after his wife died of cancer, we fell in love. My birthday was like Thanksgiving. The family and friends came and rejoiced that I was so happy. He pampered me and gave me roses and planned four trips that I would love including New York. I was living many a woman's dream. The summer of my fifty-fifth would be his sixtieth.

I planned his surprise party for his big day on July 17th. I mailed the invitations on July 3 as we left town for Dallas. On July 6 when everyone opened their mailboxes, they received the invitation. But they had already received the news that he had died suddenly the evening before. My fifty-fifth was spent in shock with my family trying to soothe my sorrow with a surprise dinner party. And friends showered me with attention throughout the day. Both were loving and welcome remedies for what ailed me. But they and I both knew I was wearing the smiling mask of normality. He and I had spoken of my birthday and he said he had a special idea in mind. I will never know what it was, but I know it would have been wonderful.

So fifty-six has come. People asked what I wanted to do. "Low key," I answered honestly. The celebration had started two weeks before with a trip to New York to see *Long Day's Journey into Night* with my sister and brother-in-law. There's nothing like a spontaneous junket to see five brilliant actors perform to get the blood stirring. "Breathtaking" is the only adequate word to describe the event, and the weekend in the city was my third in two years. But that's another story.

On my actual birthday, I went to work and chatted with colleagues, was taken to lunch by two dear friends, and I visited my son's family. It is the baby who is the gift this year. When I walked in the door, she jumped into my arms, and when I left she fretted that I was going. Needless to say, that made my day. My next stop was to visit my grand dog. Never big on pets, I have been won over totally by this hundred pound Golden Retriever that demands nothing but pours out affection along with saliva. I've gotten over the idea of being licked by a dog and enjoy his company. Then, my daughter and I set off to shop, do dinner with another friend of ours, and see a movie. Midnight found us walking her dog under a nearly full moon, and the day was over. It had been perfect. I had seen or heard from everyone to whom I matter, and therein lies the lesson. It is not the size of celebrations or even an exact date; it is the fact that we have something to celebrate. Joy is a gift from others, but happiness comes from within. It is about attitude and all those old cliches and saws: "half full glasses," "seeing stars, not mud," "wanting what you get rather than getting what you want." So, I want what I've got: family and friends, a job worth doing, and the curiosity to wonder what lies around the next bend in the road.

Pablo Neruda wrote, "Today is today with the weight of all past time." True. It is our compendium of experiences that makes us what we are, but it is the way we handle those experiences that makes us who we are. Ditch the long-planned parties. Celebrate the moment. Every day is Birth Day.

Dear Reader,

The Spirit brings us joy, but only we can create our own happiness. In the next year you are beginning there will still be moments of rage, sadness and longing. They become more bearable if we trust and keep faith.

I wish you wisdom and understanding and fortitude.

I wish you serenity.